'One of the starting points for this [book was the presentations he] gave to Café Théologiques in Walwo[rth ... which] were organised by Churches Togeth[er ... with the aim of] encouraging debate on "creative and [divisive" issues ...] also as an opportunity for ministers [new to South] London to try out ideas among Christian friends in an informal setting. Israel was one of the first I invited, partly because he was – and still is – a man willing to think about and act upon key ideas and partly because the presence of new black majority congregations can be seen as both "creative and divisive".

'Israel's presentations then and his book now display a wide knowledge of the history of Black Majority Churches, a keen awareness of where they are and what they are doing today, a good discernment of the issues they face and a challenging assessment of what those of us in the long-established churches could do. I am as ever grateful for what he has written and I warmly commend the book.'
John Richardson, Ecumenical Officer, Churches Together in South London

'In this short but significant volume, Israel Olofinjana documents developments and initiatives among BMC and highlights some of the encouraging projects that involve both BMC and Historic Churches. It becomes abundantly clear that Israel's claim that "It will now be impossible to write the history of the church in Britain without proper reference to Black Majority Churches" is both true and important, and needs to be heard. This book matters for those who share Israel's conviction that multicultural churches are a manifestation of God's kingdom on earth as a sign of a new humanity. It gives us stories of hope that this is happening even now. However, it is also an irenic and prophetic call for those in the Historic Churches to honour their brothers and sisters in BMC as equals where, tragically, this has not always been the case. As such, this book should be read by all.'
Dr Lucy Peppiatt, Principal, Westminster Theological Centre

'This is a timely and much-needed contribution to the British ecumenical landscape, and Israel Olofinjana is ideally located to be the one to make this contribution. As a member of the African Diaspora in the UK, Olofinjana is aware of the challenges faced by "migrant churches", the growth among what is known as Black Majority Churches (BMC), and the dynamic ecumenical intercultural trends on the ground – especially in London. Olofinjana's contribution will certainly mean that any current and future writing of the history of church or ecumenism in Britain must reckon with the presence of BMC! This volume will certainly help kick-start fruitful conversations on unconventional grassroots ecumenical partnerships, the complexity of the history and intra-diversity of BMC, and open up opportunities for churches to move out of the "transit lounge" of a tired kind of ecumenism. There is much here to build on and take in multiple directions!'

Rev Dr Michael N. Jagessar, writer, theologian and former moderator of the General Assembly of the United Reformed Church

'Israel Olofinjana has a vision for a British church enriched by multicultural relations for the glory of God. Here he tells the story of pioneer BMC leaders and ecumenical relations over the last century in order to develop those partnerships in the future. Engaging and succinct, this book will encourage us all to play a part in achieving this vision.'

Dr Emma Wild-Wood, Executive Director, Cambridge Centre for Christianity Worldwide

'Scarcely a week goes by without me receiving a research or book proposal, a manuscript or new book by a person of African and Caribbean heritage. This year marks the twenty-fifth anniversary of the publication of *A Time to Speak* by Paul Grant and Raj Patel that bemoaned the prevalence of external "exponents and apologists" interpreting "Black faith". They called on black Christianity to "speak" for itself. This short work is part of a developing prophetic literariness based on self-articulation from within the Black Church in Britain and I warmly welcome Rev Israel Olofinjana's latest work. I have been involved in the field of "intercultural ecumenism" for almost 20 years and it is good to see some of the developments at the intersectionality of Christian history, cultural diversity and ecumenical engagements brought together in one place. Some view the super-diversity of the Christian church as a problem, especially when that diversity has to do with culture and ethnicity. This book may help us to view such diversity differently; as an expression of God who comes to us in the persons of Father, Son and Holy Spirit and has created a church in God's image that is also diverse by nature. The challenge this work makes evident is common to any large family as it sets about living in integrity and in community. Each expression of Christianity has God-given legitimacy and we are challenged to love our sisters and brothers from expressions other than our own; because it is good and pleasant when siblings live together in unity of the kind that is so countercultural that the world believes in the source of the power that makes it possible. Rev Olofinjana has done us a great service by this exposé of the histories and intercultural activities of the British church.'

Bishop Dr Joe Aldred, Pentecostal and Multicultural Relations, Churches Together in England

'I warmly commend this latest book from Israel Olofinjana. It offers a very helpful and readable overview of multicultural ecumenical partnerships and their development and will be valuable to all Christian leaders as we sense God's call to proactively embrace diversity for the sake of the kingdom.'

Lynn Green, General Secretary, Baptist Union of Great Britain

'Contributions to world Christianity by Christians in and from Africa have been immense. These contributions benefit all Christians, no matter where they live. Theological and ecclesiastical questions that engaged the minds and experiences of Christians in ancient Egypt and Roman North Africa occupy the concerns of successive generations of Christians. They have interacted with the insights of the African Christians and adapted them to the immediate needs of local contexts. The unending varieties of Christian thoughts and expressions have also influenced African Christians through the presence and services of missionaries from outside of Africa. The modern diaspora movements of people from Africa, however, have brought back certain African elements to countries like Britain. Pastor Israel Olofinjana's present work explores how some of these elements can enhance unity and partnership between non-African Christians in the mainline churches and African Christians in Britain. It invites the readers to jointly experience the riches of multicultural Christian expressions in faith and practice. I recommend it warmly to all concerned readers and practitioners.'

Reverend Professor Daniel Jeyaraj, Professor, World Christianity & Director of Andrew Walls Centre for the Study of African and Asian Christianity, Liverpool Hope University

'Recently someone asked me what the future of the UK church looked like. I responded instantly, and with a single word: "Black". The rise of the Black Majority Churches, and their spread and growth and life and vitality, is the great untold story of British Christianity in the last three decades, and is vital to understanding the current and future shape of the church. In this book, Rev Olofinjana proves himself again one of the most capable and lucid interpreters of the BMC scene. Here he turns to ecumenical relationships, particularly to the good things that have happened between BMC and Historic Churches over the years.'

Dr Stephen Holmes, Senior Lecturer in Theology, University of St Andrews

'Not many people have been able to explore and articulate the distinctiveness and peculiarity of Black Majority and ethnic churches as Israel has clearly done in a practical and simplistic way in his book. The book could be classified as high definition that helps leaders who are dreaming of integration and how to get along with people, churches and para-churches that are vastly different from them. Israel himself has helped define integration in person, lifestyle and ministry. His experience and passion is felt throughout the book as a leader who lives a multi-ethnic life before leading a multi-ethnic church and writing a multi-ethnic book. I recommend the book both for personal and institutional enlightenment.'

Rev Yemi Adedeji, Director, One People Commission, Evangelical Alliance UK

'When I started out as a Baptist minister, nearly 30 years ago, the UK church landscape differed vastly from what it is today. Many people within church circles were and still are unaware of the monumental cultural changes taking place around them, sometimes in the same geographical community and even, sometimes, within their own churches. In the early days of my ministry, there were few people seeking to translate or interpret the diversity and significance of so-called Black Majority Church movements in and around the UK.

'The UK church continues to experience almost exponential levels of change as new communities and fresh perspectives join and contribute to the wider church scene. Thank God for people like Israel who have committed themselves to documenting the growth and impact of many of the diverse expressions of black Christianity. His work, together with that of others, dispels forever the notion that "Black Majority Churches" are on a similar evolutionary trajectory to that of White Majority Churches or that their main or sole contribution to the UK church is vibrancy, prayer and worship. This is borne out neither in theory nor in practice, and their influence is and will continue to be distinctive.

'Israel's latest offering goes the "extra mile" beyond documentation, by proposing insightful and pragmatic ways that UK Christians can further express the prophetic nature of what must inevitably be increasingly creative and diverse expressions of mission and ministry in the unfolding history of the United Kingdom.

'I look forward with anticipation to the many fresh opportunities this will surely bring about to grassroots church life.'

Rev Dr Kate Coleman, founder of Next Leadership, Baptist minister, former Chair of the Evangelical Alliance Council and a past president of the Baptist Union of Great Britain.

'African and Caribbean faith communities are now a permanent part of the British religious landscape. In these communities, church attendance is increasing rapidly while declining in many of our mainstream churches. Olofinjana's book focuses on some of these churches, outlining their history, theology and experience of ecumenism. It makes fascinating reading for those interested in understanding the growth and development of Black Majority Churches in Britain, as well as getting to grips with the diversity that exists within these churches.

'The book provides critical insights and case studies on the journey traversed by some of these churches from being "migrant sanctuaries" to churches now actively engaged in a range of social action programmes and new forms of political activism. I commend this book, not only because it makes a valuable contribution to our understanding of African and Caribbean Christianity in Britain, but also because of what the Spirit might want us to "hear", learn and do as BMC and the more established churches engage in missional partnerships and wrestle with intercultural ecumenism as authentic expressions of Christian unity.'

Dr R. David Muir, Lecturer in Ministerial Theology, Roehampton University, and Co-Chair of the National Church Leaders Forum

'It is a blessing to have this kind of book that will draw the attention of the world at large to the Black Majority Churches' ecumenical involvement in Britain. I am sure that many will be blessed by this excellent historical and educational book.

'Many books have been published with biased and incorrect narratives or data, but this book is thoroughly researched and excellently and factually presented. I therefore commend it to anyone who is keen and interested to know what ecumenism means to the Black Majority Churches and their involvement.

'I pray that the content of this book will further remind its readers about our Lord and Saviour Jesus Christ's prayer for the unity of His church and help us to accept and embrace one another in love. Amen.'

Father Olu Abiola, General Superintendent of Aladura International Church and President of Council of African and Afro-Caribbean Churches UK

Partnership in Mission

A Black Majority Church Perspective on Mission and Church Unity

Israel Olofinjana

instant
apostle

First published in Great Britain by Instant Apostle, 2015.

Instant Apostle

The Barn
1 Watford House Lane
Watford
Herts
WD17 1BJ

British Library Cataloguing-in-Publication Data

A catalogue record for this book is available from the British Library

This book and all other Instant Apostle books are available from Instant Apostle:

Website: www.instantapostle.com

E-mail: info@instantapostle.com

ISBN 978-1-909728-35-6

Printed in Great Britain

Instant Apostle is a new way of getting ideas flowing, between followers of Jesus, and between those who would like to know more about His kingdom.

It's not just about books and it's not about a one-way information flow. It's about building a community where ideas are exchanged. Ideas will be expressed at an appropriate length. Some will take the form of books. But in many cases ideas can be expressed more briefly than in a book. Short books, or pamphlets, will be an important part of what we provide. As with pamphlets of old, these are likely to be opinionated, and produced quickly so that the community can discuss them.

Well-known authors are welcome, but we also welcome new writers. We are looking for prophetic voices, authentic and original ideas, produced at any length; quick and relevant, insightful and opinionated. And as the name implies, these will be released very quickly, either as Kindle books or printed texts or both.

Join the community. Get reading, get writing and get discussing!

instant apostle

Contents

Abbreviations

ACEA	African and Caribbean Evangelical Alliance
AWUCOC	Afro-West Indian United Council of Churches
AIC	African Initiated Churches
ANPC	African New Pentecostal Churches
BCC	British Council of Churches
BMC	Black Majority Churches
BME	Black and Minority Ethnic
BMS	Baptist Missionary Society
CAACC	Council of African and Afro-Caribbean Churches
CCBI	Council of Churches in Britain and Ireland
CCP	Conference for Christian Partnership
CMS	Church Mission Society
CTBI	Churches Together in Britain and Ireland
CTE	Churches Together in England
EA	Evangelical Alliance
GDOP	Global Day of Prayer
IMCGB	International Ministerial Council of Great Britain
KICC	Kingsway International Christian Centre
LMS	London Missionary Society
MECA	Minority Ethnic Christian Affairs
NCLF	National Church Leaders Forum
NDOP	National Day of Prayer
RBG	Royal Borough of Greenwich
RCCG	Redeemed Christian Church of God
WCC	World Council of Churches

Foreword

The full history of the establishment, development and growth of the Black Majority Churches (BMC) in this country is coming together quite nicely. This book by Rev Israel Olofinjana, though not exhaustive, will contribute significantly to that history. In it he details not only the struggles the BMC faced in their establishment – for example, finding suitable places to worship, the cost of rent, cultural/liturgical differences, sharing facilities with historical churches etc – but also the struggles they are still facing today. In spite of these difficulties, the BMC are still proliferating at an extraordinary rate in British church history and in society as a whole.

In this book, Rev Olofinjana paints a bright picture in various shapes and sizes at national and local levels, all with the intention of better understanding shared mission and the expansion of the kingdom of God. The exponential growth of the BMC, particularly in London and the South East, the building of better understanding between BMC leaders and the historical churches, and the emergence of 'Spirit-led ecumenism' augurs well for what the church in Britain might look like in the future.

Rev Olofinjana is an outstanding Christian leader and author with a good understanding of what the church – the body of Christ – should be, and he writes with that conviction. This book, scholarly written, will be very useful for the theologians, church planters, social scientists and educational institutions. Those interested in ecumenical engagements, among others, should find this publication a useful resource, and I strongly recommend it.

Bishop Eric Brown, Pentecostal President of Churches Together in England

Introduction

Black Majority Churches have been in Britain for 70 years or more, depending on which year you attribute to their origins. Since their inception, they have faced many challenges including lack of church accommodation, rejection and misrepresentation. In the midst of all these factors they have grown to become one of the largest and fastest-growing church movements in Britain. It will now therefore be impossible to write the history of the church in Britain without proper reference to BMC.

How did these churches start, especially in London? They are called 'Black Majority Churches', but does this term accurately describe them? Now that we have so many BMC in the major cities of Britain, what is their mission and what kind of relationship do they have with the Historic Churches such as the Church of England and Baptists? This latter question becomes significant if we consider the fact that many BMC rent buildings from Historic Churches.

Arrangements for the hire and use of church premises have been happening since the 1960s, so what opportunities and challenges do these present for working together? Do these relationships around church buildings function merely as landlord and tenant, or is there more to them?

These are some of the questions I want to address in this short book, to give a general picture of ecumenism in Britain, and focusing particularly on important developments in London.

The purpose of this book therefore is threefold: historical, theological and ecumenical. Firstly it is to tell the story and highlight the intercultural ecumenism that is developing between BMC and Historic Churches, using London as a case study. The book considers the history of the two groups of churches working together in order to shed more light on this intercultural ecumenism. Part of this history reveals some missional ecumenism – that is, working together for the common cause of mission – but at the same time it also sheds light on some of the differences that have led to division.

While this book gives some attention to institutional ecumenism in Britain – that is, working together facilitated by ecumenical bodies and agencies – it also focuses on grassroots ecumenical partnerships that are forming between individual BMC and Historic Churches, or between two or more churches working together in a particular area in London. In the latter case, the churches working together do so around projects such as food banks, Street Pastors, prayers for the city and so on. In the case of the former, individual churches are often working together through the sharing of church buildings and resources. This book explores some of the problems encountered in the sharing of resources and offers practical suggestions as to how to work around some of the issues.

This book is written with practitioners in mind but is also relevant to scholars in the areas of mission and ecumenism. It will be of particular interest to ecumenical bodies who would like to understand more about BMC.

As the primary purpose of this book is to look at the intercultural ecumenism emerging between BMC and Historic Churches, it is important to know the history of BMC in order to fully appreciate these current developments. Part of understanding the history of BMC is to understand their mission in the UK and the journey they have travelled from being migrant repositories to churches that are trying to break out of a narrow understanding of mission. In order words, it is important to map out their mission theology. This naturally leads to the second and third purposes of the book.

The second purpose is to document the history and diversity that exists within BMC. This is done by briefly looking at their history in London. This history is not simple and straightforward, because the Black Church Movement in Britain is not homogenous but rather layered with various colours, both metaphorically and literally. This is expressed in terms of theology, ecclesiology, mission, ethnicity and culture. Therefore the term 'Black Majority Churches' does not do justice to the breadth of diversity that exists within this church movement.

The third purpose is to map out how some of these churches have journeyed from being migrant sanctuaries to churches that are now engaging in social, community and political activism. There was a time when BMC were so heavenly minded that they did not think too much about being relevant in the here and now. At other times, some BMC construed mission as primarily evangelism and church planting, but now many BMC are actively involved in social and community engagement. What theological factors have led to this shift in their understanding of mission? The prism used in this book is the language of reverse mission – that is, mission from those who used to be the beneficiaries of Western mission overseas. The term 'reverse mission' still raises a lot of questions, but how are BMC appropriating the idea to describe their mission in Britain, and what is their mission theology?

The book begins with a historical analysis of BMC, reflecting on their diversity. The second chapter explores their mission theology through the lens of reverse mission, and the third and final chapter considers the development of intercultural ecumenism between black and white churches, using London as a case study. This chapter arrangement is intentional and important because a background understanding of BMC is necessary to understand their mission. A good understanding and grounding of their history and mission helps to understand their ecumenical journey and current developments.

The information presented in this book is drawn from three sources. The material in the first chapter, which gives a concise history of BMC, using London as a framework, is drawn from a piece of research I did in 2012–13 for an Open University project on the history of BMC in London.[1] The project, which investigated different religions in London, was called *Building on History: Religion in London*. This material has been further developed for the purpose of this book, with updated information and new insights.

The second chapter is based on a paper presented at a mission conference in Bristol in 2013, themed 'Revisiting mission'. The conference was jointly organised by the Baptist Union of Great Britain, Bristol Baptist College, Church of God of Prophecy, Grace Evangelistic Ministries and West of England Baptist Association. In attendance were pastors, mission practitioners and mission theologians. This paper has since been developed and is presented here with fresh understanding and perspective.

Lastly, the material used in the third chapter on ecumenical relationships between BMC and Historic Churches began as a research paper for an ecumenical discussion in South East London called Café Theologique. Café Theologique was an initiative of Churches Together in South London under the former ecumenical officer, John Richardson. John wanted to stimulate conversations in South East London by looking at various ecumenical issues that were arising in the context of the area. People from various church traditions presented papers on different topics in a relaxed café-style atmosphere at the crypt at St Peter's Church in Walworth, South East London. The substance of chapter three was presented at one of these cafés, and also at another in North London at St Mary's Church, Putney. The comments and feedback from these gatherings have helped to reshape the paper into what it is now. In addition, the paper was presented at a postgraduate seminar at Spurgeon's

---

[1] Israel Oluwole Olofinjana, 'The History of Black Majority Churches in London'. Available at http://www.open.ac.uk/Arts/religion-in-london/resource-guides/black-majority-church.htm (accessed 21st January 2015).

College in 2013. Again, this material has been developed for the current book with new insights and updated information on ecumenical relationships and initiatives taking place in South East London.

Some clarification of terms is needed to understand what is meant in this book by Black Majority Churches and Historic Churches.

Black Majority Churches (BMC) as used in this book refers to mainly independent Pentecostal and Charismatic Churches and denominations that have originated within the black community and have a black majority congregation and leadership. These are churches that have emerged from the African and Caribbean Diaspora. It does not include BMC that are within Historic Churches.

Historic Churches as used in this book refers to churches with a longer history in comparison to independent Pentecostal BMC. These are traditional churches whose history can be traced back to the Reformation, directly or indirectly (Church of England, Baptists, Methodists, United Reformed Church and some Congregational churches), as well as churches beyond the Reformation whose identity is rooted in the Apostolic tradition and succession – for example, the Catholic Church.

Chapter one
The history and diversity of Black Majority Churches in London

Black Majority Churches or Black Multicultural Churches?

The history of BMC in London is phenomenal because within a short period of 70 years they have grown from being obscure to having great influence. Their historical development is rich and diverse in nature, which makes the generic term 'Black Majority Churches' problematic as it does not address the diversity that exists within these churches. Arlington Trotman's question two decades ago about black or black-led churches is very relevant here: he argued that the term 'black-led' or 'black church' was an imposition by outsiders and that the terminology does not satisfactorily describe these churches.[2] How outsiders have defined the Black Church over the years has not given sufficient room to explain its diversity and has led to stereotypes and misrepresentations.

There have been various theological and sociological attempts by Black and Minority Ethnic (BME) Christians to map their own conversation by defining their own identity. An example was the African and Caribbean Evangelical Alliance (ACEA) theological forum's idea to give authentic theological expression to people from black churches to speak for themselves. The initiative included people like Rev Joel

---

[2] Arlington Trotman, 'Black, Black-led or What?' in Joel Edwards, *Let's Praise Him Again: An African-Caribbean Perspective on Worship* (Eastbourne: Kingsway Publications Ltd, 1992), pp.18-34.

Edwards, then General Director of the Evangelical Alliance; Dr David Muir, then Public Theology and Policy Officer for the Evangelical Alliance; Winston Bygraves, theologian and Baptist minister; and Calvert Prentice, an Anglican minister. This theological forum was behind the production of *Let's Praise Him Again* (1992), edited by Joel Edwards and containing contributions from various church leaders and theologians.

Another example of this self-articulation of black identity is *Britain on the Brink*, a 1993 Evangelical Alliance publication tracing the sociological development of black Christian presence.[3] A third example is the publication of *A Time to Speak: Perspectives of Black Christians in Britain* (1990), edited by Paul Grant and Raj Patel. The book, as its title suggests, attempted to capture the diverse voices of black and Asian Christians in Britain.

Building on these previous works, I am articulating that BMC are diverse in terms of ecclesiology, theology, mission, ethnicity and culture. For example, some are churches while others are para-church organisations or agencies. Some are independent churches while others are part of the Historic Churches. Some are Sabbatarians while others are from Pentecostal and Holiness traditions. Some are Unitarians while others are Trinitarians. Some articulate black British theology while others preach Prosperity Gospel, and still others neither. Some have grown to become church denominations while others are still independent churches.[4] Some are plants from their denominational churches back in the Caribbean or Africa, while others are churches that have started in London and have gone on to plant churches in other parts of the world.

---

[3] Martyn Eden (ed), *Britain on the Brink* (IL, USA: Crossways Books, 1993).
[4] Some BMC are church denominations, such as the New Testament Church of God and the Redeemed Christian Church of God.

Added to this richness in theology, ecclesiology and mission is the fact that these churches have members from different nationalities and cultures. The fact that they are labelled 'black' does not mean that everyone attending these churches is identical. Take, for example, New Wine Church in Woolwich: the fact that Africans attend the church does not mean they are all the same, as Africa after all is not just a country but a continent comprising many different countries! The church is also diverse in terms of the age and socio-economic status of the people who attend. To an outsider, the church might appear to be 'black', but in reality it is a multicultural, multi-ethnic intergenerational church.

In view of these elements of diversity, the argument can be made that some BMC should instead be labelled Black Multicultural Churches, as this would represent their increasing diversity. However, I am aware that we still have mono-ethnic BMC, where one nationality or culture dominates.

Pioneers of Black Majority Churches

As the capital of the UK, London has played a fascinating role in the history and emergence of BMC. There is a concentration of BMC in London and in other major cities such as Bristol, Birmingham, Liverpool, Leeds, Manchester and Edinburgh, for several reasons. In the case of London, one obvious factor is that as the capital city of the former British Empire, and currently that of the Commonwealth, it is well known in Africa and the Caribbean. This goes back to times of slavery and colonialism. Another reason is that London is often one of the first points of entry into the UK, because of its seaport in the past and its airports in the modern era, which means that it is easily accessible to immigrants. As a major global and cultural city, London also offers job opportunities and an enticing multicultural environment compared to rural areas. Also, as a result of the diaspora effect, new immigrants often join social and family networks already in existence.

The unique role that London plays in the history of BMC includes the fact that the first black Pentecostal church in Britain was founded there.[5] This was Sumner Road Chapel founded by Rev Thomas Kwame Brem-Wilson in Peckham in 1906. Rev Brem-Wilson, a businessman and schoolmaster, was born into a wealthy family in Dixcove, Ghana in around 1855. He migrated to Britain in 1901 and later founded Sumner Road Chapel in Peckham, which is known today as Sureway International Christian Ministries in its new location of Herne Hill, South East London. Rev Brem-Wilson's church was an African Pentecostal church, although he was also involved with the origins of the Pentecostal movement in Britain. This was largely because of his friendships with the likes of Alexander Boddy (the Anglican priest who is recognised as the father of British Pentecostalism), Cecil Polhill (one of the pioneers of the Pentecostal missionary movement in Britain), D. P. Williams and W. J. Williams (founders of the Apostolic Church in Britain).[6]

---

[5] However, this may not have been the first BMC in Britain. That honour goes to a church founded by John Jea in the early nineteenth century. After a fruitful itinerant ministry in North America and Europe, John settled down in Portsmouth with his wife, and they may have started a church in their house in around 1805–15. See John Jea, *The Life, History and Unparalleled Sufferings of John Jea, The African Preacher* (Cornwall: Dodo Press, 2009).

[6] Babatunde Adedibu, *Coat of Many Colours* (London: Wisdom Summit, 2012), p.26, Israel Olofinjana, *Turning the Tables on Mission: Stories of Christians from the Global South in the UK* (Watford: Instant Apostle, 2013), p.119. See also Israel Olofinjana, 'The First African Pentecostal Church in Europe (1906–Present)', May 2012. Available at http://israelolofinjana.wordpress.com/2012/05/06/the-first-african-pentecostal-church-in-europe-1906-present/ (accessed 22nd January 2015).

The next phase of the history of BMC in London was the founding of the League of Coloured Peoples by Dr Harold Moody. Although this was not a church, it functioned as a para-church agency, catering for the welfare needs of black people and other ethnic minorities.

Harold Moody was born in Jamaica in 1882 and came to London in 1908 to pursue a career in medicine. He studied at King's College Hospital in London and qualified as a medical doctor. Frustrated at the lack of opportunities to practise medicine, he turned his attention to the medical needs of black people in Peckham. To this end, and being convinced by his Christian faith, he started the League of Coloured People on 13th March 1931 at the central YMCA in Tottenham Court Road. Dr Moody was also actively involved in mission as he was a deacon at Camberwell Congregational Church, a leading member and later president of the London Missionary Society (LMS), and the president of the London Confederation of the Christian Endeavour Union.[7]

The planting of Caribbean Pentecostal and Holiness Churches

The 1940s and 1950s saw an influx of Caribbean families into the UK following the invitation by the British government to come and help rebuild the country after the devastation of the Second World War. Many people from the Caribbean responded to this call, but to their surprise and dismay they found that they were excluded by both society and the church. The majority of the people from the Caribbean regarded themselves as British citizens and as part of the Commonwealth, and therefore expected to be treated equally. But they soon realised, on seeing posters making such statements as, 'No Irish, No Blacks and No

---

[7] Mark Sturge, *Look What the Lord has Done* (Milton Keynes: Scripture Union, 2005), p.73.

24

Dogs', that the wealth was in fact not common at all, and that they were regarded as second-class citizens. This rejection, combined with other important factors such as loyalty to church brands, led to the formation of Caribbean Pentecostal and Holiness Churches. For example, Joe Aldred articulated that the New Testament Church of God was founded because its members from the Caribbean had not found their denomination in operation in Britain, and therefore established it themselves.[8]

Another factor for the establishment of new churches was the perceived 'coldness' of British Christianity that some experienced when they attended British churches. The quiet, reflective style of worship was very different to the expressive style of Pentecostals, which is even more pronounced in an African–Caribbean culture.

Lastly, the call of mission to the UK led to the formation of churches, as we will see from the example of Philip Mohabir in chapter two.

This period of the 1940s and 1950s is commonly referred to as the Windrush generation, named after the ship, the SS Empire Windrush, which brought approximately 493 people from the Caribbean on 22nd June 1948 to Tilbury in London. The first of the Caribbean Pentecostal Churches founded in the UK was Calvary Church of God in Christ, which started in London in 1948. The church became affiliated with Church of God in Christ, USA, in 1952 and has 21 church plants in the UK at the time of writing. Other churches soon followed, such as the New Testament Church of God (1953), Church of God of Prophecy (1953) and Wesleyan Holiness Church (1958). The New Testament Assembly, founded in London in 1961, numbers 18 churches in Britain at the time of writing. The first New Testament Church of God (NTCG) in London was founded in

---

[8] Joe Aldred, *Respect: Understanding Caribbean British Christianity* (Peterborough: Epworth Publishing, 2005), p.92.

the Hammersmith area in 1959 (NTCG has 128 churches in the UK at the time of writing).

It was also during the 1950s that the renowned late Guyanese missionary Philip Mohabir came to Britain. Philip arrived in 1956 and started an itinerant ministry in Brixton which included preaching in shops, in pubs, on buses and from house to house. He also planted churches both in London and outside London and later pioneered the founding of the West Indian Evangelical Alliance (WIEA) in 1984. The WIEA was later known as the African Caribbean Evangelical Alliance (ACEA), which has now stopped operating. Philip's pioneering missionary work will be analysed in chapter two, and there are more details about the work of the ACEA in chapter three.

African Initiated Churches in Britain[9]

The independence of African countries, starting with Ghana in 1957, led to African diplomats, students and tourists coming to Britain. They discovered, like the Caribbeans before them, that they were rejected by the British churches and society at large. Combined with a missionary intent, this rejection led to the formation of African Initiated Churches (AIC) in London. The first of such churches to be planted was the Church of the Lord Aladura (Aladura) planted in 1964 by the late Primate Adeleke Adejobi, assisted by Rev Father Olu Abiola, in South London. This church has its headquarters (HQ) in Nigeria. Others soon followed, such as the Cherubim and Seraphim Church in 1965

---

[9] AIC are also referred to as African Independent Churches, African Instituted Churches and African Indigenous Churches. They are churches that started in Africa at the beginning of the twentieth century through renewal and reacting against European Christianity that the Mission Churches introduced into Africa. They are churches that indigenised Christianity among Africans by developing African cultural forms of worship.

(HQ in Nigeria), the Celestial Church of Christ in 1967 (HQ also in Nigeria), Aladura International Church founded in London by Rev Father Olu Abiola in 1970, Christ Apostolic Church (CAC) Mount Bethel founded by Apostle Ayo Omideyi in 1974 (HQ in Lagos, Nigeria), Christ Apostolic Church (CAC) of Great Britain in 1976 (HQ in Ibadan, Nigeria), and Born Again Christ Healing Church founded in London by Bishop Fidelia Onyuku-Opukiri in 1979.

The first of the Ghanaian AIC to arrive in England was the Divine Prayer Society by Archbishop Owusu Akuffo in the early 1960s, followed by the Musama Disco Christo Church (MDCC) by Rev Dr Jeri Jehu-Appiah.[10] Both churches are based in London.

New-generation Caribbean Pentecostal Churches

Since the 1990s there have emerged New-generation Caribbean Pentecostal Churches. I refer to these churches as 'New-generation' because they appeal to Caribbean British Christians who are second and third generation. They also have a wider appeal to other nationalities. Many of their leaders are second- or third-generation Caribbean British Christians. These churches are Pentecostal, have dynamic worship and worship teams, use the gifts of the Holy Spirit and have creative preaching styles. They are very proactive in terms of community and social engagement, providing services such as food banks, debt counselling, soup kitchens, prison ministries and homeless shelters. Examples of these churches are:

---

[10] Afe Adogame, 'African Christian Communities in Diaspora', in Ogbu Kalu (eds), *African Christianity* (Trenton, NJ: African World Press, 2007), pp.435-436. Israel Olofinjana, *Reverse in Ministry and Mission: Africans in the Dark Continent of Europe*, (Milton Keynes: Author House, 2010), pp.35-41.

- Ruach Ministries, led by Bishop John Francis (1994)[11]

- Rhema Christian Ministries (1996), formerly known as Croydon Rhema Fellowship (1990), founded by Pastor Mark Goodridge and now led by Pastor Marva Scott

- Christian Life City (1996), led by Bishop Wayne Malcolm

- Micah Christian Ministries (1998), led by Pastor Denis Wade

- The Tabernacle Church, led by Pastor Michael W. White[12]

- Greater Faith Ministries, led by Bishop Lennox Hamilton[13]

African New Pentecostal Churches 1980s–1990s

In the 1980s and 1990s there emerged a new type of African church. Such churches are termed African New Pentecostal Churches (ANPC). It is the proliferation of these churches, particularly in the 1990s, that has drawn the attention of scholars and recently the media to BMC. There follow the profiles and information of some of these churches, to offer a snapshot of who they are.

Deeper Life Bible Church, started by Pre Ovia in London in 1985, now has more than 40 branch churches in the UK. The church recently purchased a former cinema building in St John's Hill, Clapham Junction in London. The multi-purpose building has been fully refurbished into a modern auditorium with the capacity to seat 2,500 people.

---

[11] Bishop John Francis' father, Bishop Tesley Francis, founded the First Born Church of the Living God in the 1960s.
[12] Michael White's father founded this church in the 1950s with the name The Bible Way Church of the Lord Jesus Christ Apostolic.
[13] Olofinjana, *Reverse in Ministry and Mission*, p.41.

New Covenant Church was founded by Rev Dr Paul Jinadu in Nigeria in 1985. The church started in the UK in 1986 and now has more than 41 church plants in the UK. Their UK national overseer is Rev Obafemi Omisade.

The Church of Pentecost started in Ghana around 1937 through the efforts of one of the Apostolic Church missionaries, James McKeown. It began in London in collaboration with Elim Pentecostal Churches around 1988–89. Today it has more than 82 branch churches in the UK in major cities such as London, Birmingham, Manchester, Liverpool, Nottingham, Cardiff, Leicester, Sheffield, Leeds and Glasgow.

The Redeemed Christian Church of God (RCCG) was started in London in 1988 by David Okunade and Ade Okerende. RCCG now boasts more than 700 churches in Britain, making it one of the largest and fastest-growing church denominations in Britain.

Beneficial Veracious Christ Church (BVC) was founded in London in 1988 by Archbishop J. P. Hackman. Bishop Hackman is the president of Trans-Atlantic and Pacific Alliance of Churches (TAPAC), an ecumenical body for African Diaspora churches in Britain. This includes West, East and Central African churches. TAPAC is one of the member organisations of Churches Together in England.

Christ Faith Tabernacle was started by Apostle Alfred Williams in Deptford in 1989 as a house fellowship. It had its first official service in March 1990 at All Saints Church in New Cross. Later the church relocated to a bigger property in New Cross which is now its international headquarters, Bethesda Building. The church now has a cathedral in Woolwich (Ebenezer Building), having bought an old Gothic theatre building, and it celebrated its silver jubilee in 2015.

Christian Victory Group was started by Pastor Ade Omooba in 1991 as a relief initiative for homeless people in London. It was registered in 1992 as a Christian para-church charity organisation. Its work includes the provision of education for children and young people, medical relief to developing countries, the provision of homes for the homeless, and training, consultancy and support to other Christian or voluntary groups who are involved in helping the poor. The Christian Victory Group also has a church arm. Pastor Ade is a co-founder of the Christian Legal Centre (CLC) and Christian Concern for our Nation (CCFON): both are Christian organisations that assist marginalised Christians to have a voice in the public square. They also assist in fighting discrimination against Christians in the workplace through legal representation and advocacy.

Kingsway International Christian Centre (KICC) was founded by Matthew Ashimolowo in London in 1992. KICC became the largest church in the UK around 1998 when it launched its church facility in Hackney, which was reported to be able to seat 5,000 people comfortably. KICC has now relocated to a new 24-acre site in Buckmore Park, Maidstone in Kent. This new site is designated 'Prayer City' and services are held there, as well as at their Land of Wonders in Hoe Street, Walthamstow, London.

New Wine Church was founded by the late Dr Tayo Adeyemi in 1993 in Woolwich, London. New Wine Church is one of the largest churches in the UK, and is now led by Pastor Michael Olawore. It has a membership of around 3,000 people. Since 2002 the church has been running a Christmas Hamper Campaign, and it is estimated that approximately 124,500 people have benefited from this initiative.[14]

---

[14] New Wine Church Brochure, 2015.

World Harvest Christian Centre (WHCC) was founded in London by Pastor Wale Babatunde in 1995. The church has planted in other parts of the UK such as Bolton, Manchester and Southend. WHCC has also established church plants outside the UK in places such as Liberia, Benin, Nigeria and Canada. The church has a Bible college which trains men and women for mission and has also established the Christian Heritage and Reformation Trust, an initiative that seeks to foster social reformation and revival in Britain. Pastor Wale believes that Britain is in need of revival and he has authored three books on the subject, warning the church in Britain to wake up and seek God. The three books are *Great Britain has Fallen: How to Restore Britain's Greatness as a Nation* (2002), *Awake Great Britain: A Call to the Church to Rise out of Slumber* (2005) and *Great Men and Women who made Great Britain* (2013). I must caution that not every African Christian in Britain agrees or shares Pastor Babatunde's views of Britain;[15] nevertheless, his books, although controversial and critical, serve as an example of theological reflections of an African pastor on the nature of post-Christian secular Britain.

Mountain of Fire and Miracle (MFM) was founded in Nigeria in 1989 by Dr Daniel Olukoya. This church started in London in 1996 and there are now more than 80 church plants all over the UK.

African New Pentecostal Churches from 2000 to the present

Since the millennium there has been an unprecedented increase in the number of ANPC in the UK. One example is Winners

---

[15] Harvey Kwiyani, *Sent Forth: African Missionary Work in the West* (New York: Orbis Books, 2014), p.101.

Chapel, founded in Nigeria by the controversial Bishop David Oyedepo Sr in 1981. Bishop Oyedepo Sr has been named the richest church minister in Nigeria after being estimated to have assets worth £93 million, including more than two private jets and a Rolls-Royce Phantom. Winners Chapel planted its first church in the UK in Bermondsey, London, in 2001. The church has now relocated to a new building in Dartford. It is led by Pastor David Oyedepo Jr (Bishop Oyedepo's son) and has a growing membership of about 3,000 people. It has other church plants in Surrey, Middlesex and Luton. In addition, it has branch churches in Manchester, Birmingham, Leeds, Bradford, Liverpool, Glasgow, Dublin and Brussels.

In 2012 the UK Charity Commission, concerned that some church funds were being remitted to the church headquarters back in Nigeria, conducted an investigation of the church following £16.7 million of donations from its British members. The usual practice of Winners Chapel is that its branch churches across the world send financial contributions to the church headquarters in Lagos, Nigeria. This practice was not fully understood by the UK Charity Commission, who decided to investigate the situation, given that and other concerns. Added to the situation is the reputation of the founding bishop as a Prosperity preacher. In July 2015, the Charity Commission released a report concluding that it had found no evidence of misappropriation of funds and that the minor discrepancies had been explained and resolved by the charity's trustees.[16]

Another church that has had its share of controversy is Christ Embassy, originally founded in Nigeria by Chris Oyakhilome. The church began in London around the year 2000 and now has

---

[16] Daniel Farey-Jones, 'No evidence of wrongdoing found at Christian charity, regulator's report reveal', *Third Sector*. Available at http://www.thirdsector.co.uk/no-evidence-wrongdoing-found-christian-charity-regulators-report-reveals/governance/article/1356226 (accessed 20th July 2015).

more than 22 churches in London and 16 outside of London. The church was the subject of a Charity Commission investigation in 2014 for financial mismanagement. The investigation happened to coincide with Oyakhilome's marriage breakdown after his wife filed for a divorce.[17]

Allegations of and investigations into financial mismanagement and family breakdown in these churches carries negative publicity and damages the image of BMC. This often leads to bad press and stereotyping of BMC by the media. While leaders of BMC, like all ministers of the gospel, have a duty and responsibility to have financial and marital integrity to avoid such negative press, and to follow the model of Jesus as a servant leader, the media also have a responsibility to get their facts right and not stereotype. The majority of BMC have good financial accountability and management, and the majority of BMC pastors are not involved in marital scandals.

A trip to Old Kent Road or Woolwich, both in South East London, reveals the rate of proliferation of African churches in the UK. The Being Built Together project, a research work into the history, demographics and ecclesiology of BMC in the borough of Southwark, estimates that there are about 252 BMC in that borough.[18] Lewisham and many other inner-city boroughs are also experiencing this increase in the number of BMC. For example, in 2013, of the 275 churches in the borough

[17] 'Christ Embassy Under Investigation for Alleged Financial Mismanagement and Divorce on the Cards for Christ Embassy Founders?' *Keep the Faith* magazine, issue 89, 2014, p.7.
[18] 'Being Built Together: A Story of New Black Majority Churches in the London Borough of Southwark', Being Built Together Final Report June 2013, a joint research work by Roehampton University, Southwark for Jesus and Churches Together in South London.

of Lewisham, it was estimated that about 100 were BMC.[19] One question that needs to be asked is, why do we have a concentration of ANPC in one location, so that it is possible to have five Nigerian churches in one area or using one building? Is this God's mission or is it rather competition? This is now becoming a problem in many London boroughs such as Lewisham, Greenwich and Southwark, and some of these churches are also using industrial estates and buildings that are not classified for church use.[20]

While BMC are proliferating, it is difficult to accurately estimate their numbers in London as many are either not registered as charities or are unknown. In addition, the use of Historic Church buildings, or even a pastor's front room, makes it difficult to keep track of the numbers. This makes researching into BMC histories problematic. On the other hand, some BMC like to be known as international churches (even if they only have one church branch), and are therefore making their history available through their websites and other printed media.

In addition, oral history in the form of testimonies plays a vital role in telling their stories. Pastors and founders who are now leading so-called successful mega churches often like to tell the stories of how the church started with one or two people in their living room and how it has grown in numbers. This is done in appreciation to God, who is seen as the reason for the success and growth. These oral stories are worth paying attention to by researchers and observers, even if the facts may be slightly exaggerated or embellished.

As BMC continue to multiply every day with new visions and new grand names, what is their mission, and what relationships

---

[19] This estimate was based on me going round counting BMC in the borough and matching it against the official data from Lewisham Council.
[20] This is one of the reasons why Being Built Together was set up, to investigate how BMC use some of these buildings.

exist between these churches and British Historic Churches? Their mission in Britain will be explored in chapter two.

Chapter two

From migrant sanctuaries towards structural change: Mapping the theological shift in reverse mission of BMC in the UK

The journey of BMC in Britain as nuanced and described in chapter one can be expressed as from obscurity to emergence. Seventy years ago, people were neither really aware even of the existence of these churches nor knew what they were about, but today some are celebrated and their contributions recognised in society as many BMC leaders have received OBEs, MBEs and other honours. In addition, the mission of BMC used to be understood primarily as evangelism, but that is changing, and many BMC are now engaging in social and community activism. Some are taking a further step and are engaging in systemic and structural issues. An example is the current involvement of BMC in the Human Trafficking and Modern-day Slavery Bill.[21]

What are the theological contours that mark this transition? Part of the story of BMC in the UK is the shift that has taken place in world Christianity (reverse mission being a major implication). The unfolding drama of missionaries and pastors from former mission fields now ministering in Europe and North America is becoming a phenomenon that is attracting the attention of both academics and the media. Among scholars of religion and mission practitioners the question remains: Is

---

[21] The government held a consultation with BMC leaders and activists on the Human Trafficking and Modern-day Slavery Bill on 10th March 2015. I was one of the leaders in attendance.

reverse mission a rhetoric or a reality?[22] In other words, can we say reverse mission is taking place when, for example, a Nigerian pastor is leading a Nigerian church in London? A different but related question is whether reverse mission is only validated when an ethnic pastor is leading a white congregation. Lastly, what is the goal of reverse mission? Is it only about evangelising white people, or is it also about the planting and building of ethnic mega churches?

Reverse mission and pioneers of BMC

It is important to start with the definition of reverse mission. Matthew Ojo, an African Church historian and theologian, defined it as:

> The sending of missionaries to Europe and North America by churches and Christians from the non-Western world, particularly Africa, Asia, Latin America, which were at the receiving end of Catholic and Protestant missions as mission fields from the sixteenth century to the late twentieth century.[23]

In this definition, Ojo highlights the shift in the geography and direction of mission from the South to the North. He also

---

[22] Azonkah Ukah, 'Reverse Mission or Asylum Christianity? A Nigerian Church in Europe', in Toyin Falola and Augustine Agwuele, (eds), *Africans and the Politics of Popular Culture* (Rochester: University of Rochester Press, 2009), pp.104-132. Richard Burgess, 'Bringing Back the Gospel: Reverse Mission among Nigerian Pentecostals in Britain', *Journal of Religion in Europe*, 4 (3), 2011, pp.429-449. Babatunde Adedibu, 'Reverse Mission or Migrant Sanctuaries? Migration, Symbolic Mapping, and Missionary Challenges of Britain's Black Majority Churches', *Pneuma*, 35 (3), 2013, pp.405-423.
[23] Matthew Ojo, 'Reverse Mission', in Jonathan J. Bonk (ed), *Encyclopedia of Mission and Missionaries* (NY: Routledge, 2007), p.380.

mentions the intentionality of mission by the sending of missionaries from the Majority World.[24] While the sending of missionaries from the South is vital and marks a theological shift, it must however be pointed out that there are those who have migrated for other reasons and have ended up planting churches and doing mission in Britain. These other factors include economic, political, educational and social reasons. A good example of those who have migrated for other reasons but have ended up doing mission in Britain is the migration of the Caribbeans to the UK in the 1940s to the 1960s.

The Caribbean migration of the 1940s (as detailed in chapter one) was met with rejection, which became one of the reasons some BMC were founded. Joel Edwards and Mark Sturge have observed that the founding of Caribbean churches was partly a response to the spiritual, economic, social and cultural needs of the Caribbean community which otherwise would have gone unmet.[25] These churches became migrant sanctuaries and helped to sustain and nurture the identity and spiritual well-being of black and ethnic minority people in a difficult and often hostile environment.

Can the planting of these churches be regarded as reverse mission? This is a difficult question because those early pioneers responded to God's call in an environment that was far from welcoming. The founding of the Caribbean Pentecostal and Holiness churches can be viewed as the first stage of reverse mission, as they laid the foundation and paved the way for what was to follow. In many ways, the Caribbean churches paid the price for the success that African churches later enjoyed.

---

[24] Africa, Asia, South America and the Caribbean.
[25] Interview with Joel Edwards on 15th February 2011 and with Mark Sturge on 8th March 2011.

Towards a theology of reverse mission

While Ojo's definition of reverse mission highlights some of the essentials of the idea, my own understanding is somewhat different. Reverse mission, although a controversial term and not accepted by all African theologians, is one example of mission practice and is an emerging theme in mission studies.[26] It stems from a sense of humility and gratitude, acknowledging that those of us who come from former mission fields are directly or indirectly the spiritual fruits of European mission. It recognises that mission is no longer the privilege of the Western church but is now carried out from everywhere to everywhere, and that those of us from the Majority World have something to contribute to mission theology and its practice. Therefore, both those intentionally sent and those migrating for other reasons (economic, educational and social factors) come to reach out through holistic mission (evangelism, healing and social action) to the different peoples (indigenes as well as other nationalities) of the Western world.

This chapter will continue to examine this definition and will offer examples to illustrate the points mentioned. It is important to note from the above definition that reverse mission recognises and appreciates the spiritual blessings Christianity brought to places such as Africa and the Caribbean. This is why Pastor Kingsley Appaigyei, a Ghanaian Baptist minister who leads one of the largest Baptist churches in Britain, observed that African Christians ministering in the UK are directly or indirectly a harvest of the seeds sown by the early missionaries to Africa.[27] This definition also recognises migratory factors that aid reverse

---

[26] Springdale College in Birmingham is about to start teaching reverse mission as one of the modules of its Master's degree in Missional Leadership.

[27] Cited in Olofinjana, *Reverse in Mission*, p.2.

mission, but more importantly it is the bold claim that reverse mission is merely one example of mission.

This raises lot of questions, not least what we mean by mission. Mission is defined by Howard Peskett and Vinoth Ramachandra as:

> Mission is not primarily about going. It is about being a distinctive kind of people, a countercultural, multinational community among the nations. It is modelling before a sceptical world what the living God of the Bible really is like. Whether we remain all our lives in the towns of our birth or travel to the slums of Calcutta or the wastelands of Madison Avenue, we are all called to mission. For mission is to put our lives on the cutting edge where God is at work.[28]

Two things are important from this definition for our investigations in this chapter: firstly that mission is seen as God's work (*missio Dei*), and secondly that it involves every Christian.

First is the understanding that God is missional. It was mission that led God to create the world in the first place. This was also played out in the Old Testament by God revealing Himself through the children of Israel to the other nations (Genesis 22:17-18; Exodus 19:6, mirrored in 1 Peter 2:9). It was this understanding that also saw God send Jesus, His only son, to redeem humanity. The redemptive work continued through the work of the Holy Spirit in the church, as we see in the Acts of the Apostles. In essence, the Triune God is a missionary! If Jesus, the head of the church, is a missionary, His body must be a missionary people (1 Corinthians 12:12-31). It is from within this understanding that the church must see her mission. We are to join in with God's mission and not to ask Him to join in ours.

---

[28] Howard Peskett and Vinoth Ramachandra, *The Message of Mission* (Downers Grove, IL: Inter-Varsity Press, 2003), p.123.

One implication of this is that just as some European missionaries heard God's call to go to Africa, Asia, South America and the Caribbean, so are these former recipients now hearing the same God calling them back to Europe. The same God who called some European missionaries is the same God who is calling missionaries from the Caribbean and Africa, and sometimes this call comes after people have already migrated for completely different reasons! God uses incredible and often difficult circumstances to commission His people graciously in His world.

The implication of the second point, that mission involves every Christian, is that mission cannot be the prerogative of the Western church alone, but it is also the call to the global church to actively participate in God's plan. It is God who calls and sends people to anywhere He wants them to serve, whether local or global. The world is God's mission field; therefore Europe as well as Africa is a mission field.

Philip Mohabir's calling to Britain as a missionary in 1956 reflects this view of mission as from anywhere to everywhere. He can be regarded as one of the pioneers of reverse mission. The brilliance of Philip's story was the fact that he was not sent by a church or mission agency but by his Hindu family, who did not have a clue why he was travelling to Britain. Nevertheless, Philip saw himself as a missionary called and sent by God from Guyana to Britain.[29]

How can we ascertain that Philip was called by God and that he was involved in God's mission? The example of Jesus as a suffering servant called by God is one way of testing a call from God. Jesus was called by God, yet He came to us in weakness, poverty and brokenness. Philip suffered a lot for answering God's call. Many times he slept on the streets of London because

[29] Philip Mohabir, *Building Bridges* (London: Hodder & Stoughton, 1988), pp.37-39. Also see Israel Oluwole Olofinjana, *Turning the Tables on Mission*.

he had no money and no one to turn to when he arrived. He had a successful ministry preaching in public spaces, and later planted several churches. In addition, as we will see in chapter three, his ministry was not limited to ethnic minorities; indeed, his vision was to see black and white Christians working together in partnership.

Here we can draw some practical lessons from Philip in that while he did not neglect the socio-economic needs of his own people, he also ensured that his ministry reached other people in society. Some of the congregations he helped to found are multicultural churches, and some of the leaders he mentored are today ministering in multicultural contexts. Two examples are Joel Edwards, the International Director of Micah Challenge, and Mark Sturge, London Regional Coordinator for Christian Aid.

Philip Mohabir's story illustrates that not all Caribbeans came as economic migrants; rather some came to Britain with the intention of mission. His example marks a theological shift in seeing Britain as a mission field rather than one that only sends missionaries. This turning point in the understanding of mission was further developed in the 1980s when many African pastors were sent to plant churches or extend churches in Britain, for a variety of reasons.

The sending of African pastors and the rise of mono-ethnic churches

The 1980s witnessed African Pentecostal Churches sending pastors and missionaries to Britain to plant churches. Some of these church plants were more about gathering scattered church members who resided in Britain than a new expression of church based on this new context of ministry. Matthew Ashimolowo was sent by Foursquare Gospel Church in Nigeria in 1984, which had over a period of many years seen many of its members travel to the UK. These church members were asking for a branch of Foursquare Gospel Church Nigeria to be planted in London and requested a pastor. Matthew Ashimolowo was sent in response to this. In 1992, after about eight years of leading the church, Ashimolowo left Foursquare Gospel Church to start an independent work, known today as Kingsway International Christian Centre (KICC).

Pre Ovia was sent by the Deeper Life Bible Church in Nigeria in 1985. This was also as a result of a significant number of Deeper Life Church members having relocated to the UK.

Lastly, New Covenant Church in Nigeria sent Titus David (deceased) in 1986 to start New Covenant Church.[30]

The churches that grew from these church plants were mainly mono-ethnic churches – that is, churches with one dominant ethnicity or nationality. Some critics, such as Paul Freston, ask whether reverse mission is really being attempted considering that the majority of these churches are only reaching people from their own nationalities?[31] While this is a valid criticism, it also has to be said that some of the African pastors sent in the 1980s made attempts to reach out beyond their nationalities. It is worth mentioning the efforts of the late Titus David of New Covenant Church who saw his task as not of gathering but of planting. David saw himself as a missionary to England and therefore wanted the church in Britain to become vibrant. He had taken time to gather some information about British culture, which helped him to adapt and adjust. David also sought to bring together other Nigerian ministers through the Nigerian Ministers Fellowship that he started, but after a while he came to

---

[30] Hugh Osgood, *African Neo-Pentecostal Churches and British Evangelicalism 1985-2005: Balancing Principles and Practicalities*, unpublished PhD, School of Oriental and African Studies, University of London, 2006, pp.95-98.

[31] Paul Freston, 'Reverse Mission: A Discourse in Search of Reality?' in *PentecoStudies: An Interdisciplinary Journal for Research on the Pentecostal and Charismatic Movements*, Vol 9, No 10 (Sheffield: Equinox Publishing, 2010), pp.158-159.

the conclusion that this fellowship was too exclusive and would not help the mission of the Nigerian churches in the UK.

David later came across the West Indian Evangelical Alliance (WIEA) which later changed its name to the Afro-Caribbean Evangelical Alliance. David was one of the people who pushed for the name change from Afro-Caribbean to the African and Caribbean Evangelical Alliance (ACEA) in order to reflect and include African churches. Despite the fact that David was actively involved as an executive of ACEA, he was still not satisfied with the separation of black and white churches. He networked with white British evangelical leaders and formed a meaningful partnership with Colin Urquhart of Kingdom Faith Ministries. David later left New Covenant Church to plant a new church with the name Christ Family Church. Part of his reason for leaving New Covenant Church was his desire to plant a multicultural church, although it must be mentioned that Christ Family Church ended up being a predominantly Nigerian church.[32]

It appears that the gathering of former church members to start churches in the UK led to many African mono-ethnic churches. It must, however, be mentioned that we also have white mono-ethnic churches where the majority of the congregation are white British, English, Welsh, Scottish or Irish.

How are some African Pentecostal churches responding to change the pattern of African mono-ethnic churches?

Collaborative mission: BMC and British Pentecostals and Charismatics

In this and the following sections I will consider how some BMC have responded to change the pattern of mono-ethnic churches. These attempts are still in progress and have not been

---

[32] Osgood, *African Neo-Pentecostal Churches and British Evangelicalism 1985-2005*, pp.110-112.

completely successful yet, but they are the reasons why in my definition of reverse mission I mention the intention to reach out to different people in the West.

Some African Pentecostal churches, in their effort to break the pattern of being mono-ethnic churches, decided to work in partnership with British churches. One of these is the Church of Pentecost from Ghana, which planted its first church in Britain in 1988. In 1994 it became the Elim Church of Pentecost through affiliating with Britain's Elim Foursquare Alliance. The church created two types of service in order to reach out to white British as well as to those from the Ghanaian culture. One service was primarily for those ethnic minorities who wanted to have a church where they could speak their local languages, such as Twi, and be free to express their culture. The other church service was an international time of worship, conducted in English and ensuring that culture was expressed in a way that did not hinder other people from attending the church.[33] These exciting experiments were partially successful, as the church managed to attract nationalities other than Ghanaians.

Another example of an African Pentecostal church that has worked in partnership with other British evangelicals is the Deeper Life Bible Church. In 2009, it organised a conference called 'Fresh Focus', which brought together black and white churches. The conference witnessed speakers from British evangelical streams and African Pentecostal churches sharing platforms. Speakers included Roger Forster, founder of Ichthus Christian Fellowship; Hugh Osgood, founder of Cornerstone Christian Centre; Apostle Alfred Williams, founder of Christ Faith Tabernacle, London; and W. F. Kumuyi, founder of Deeper

---

[33] The history and mission strategy of the Church of Pentecost in the UK was recounted by the chair of the church, Dr Opoku-Onyinah, at a mission conference, Missio Africanus, on 27th June 2014 at Birmingham Christian College. I was present at the conference as one of the speakers.

Life Bible Church, Nigeria. These partnerships with British indigenous churches are important, firstly because they highlight that while pastors and missionaries from Africa sense a call to the UK, they are becoming more aware that they cannot do mission on their own. Secondly, partnering with a British church helps them to understand the British culture and how to contextualise mission. Partnership will be discussed in greater detail in chapter three, but these attempts at collaboration in mission mark another theological shift in the discourse of reverse mission.

From the attractional model of church to incarnational missional communities

While some BMC are working in collaborative mission, others are making attempts to learn about their new context of ministry through missional church conversations. This is the case with Pastor Lincoln Serwanga, Senior Pastor of Liberty Christian Fellowship in Camberwell, London, and with Pastor Akosua Arkhurst, Senior Pastor of the Word Church in Peckham. They both trained at the International Bible Institute of London (IBIOL) run by Kensington Temple (KT) in the early 1990s, and after completing their studies planted their respective churches under the auspices of Kensington Temple. But despite this cross-cultural training, Lincoln's church remained predominantly a Ugandan church while Akosua's remained predominantly a Ghanaian church. This raised a lot of questions and led them to begin a series of conversations with white evangelical church leaders (who were also tired of the attractional model of church) in the borough of Southwark about how to transition to missional communities that would result in reaching different people in their respective neighbourhoods.[34]

---

[34] These conversations started about three years ago and are led by Phil Stokes, leader of the Well Church in Camberwell, London, in

In a separate development, Springdale College and the Redeemed Christian Church of God (RCCG) ran a pilot scheme in 2014 to train RCCG pastors in an intensive one-year course on missional leadership. This was the brainchild of Babatunde Adedibu, the RCCG theologian who is keen for the RCCG to develop missional leadership that will move the denomination from being attractional to missional. Part of the training was delivered by Rev David Wise, Senior Pastor of Greenford Baptist Church, a multicultural, multi-ethnic Baptist church in North West London, and also by Dr Harvey Kwiyani, founding director of Missio Africanus and one of the directors of the Centre for Missionaries from the Majority World.

Why are these missional church conversations important? Churches in Britain must shift from expecting non-Christians to turn up at our church services or activities to finding creative ways of engaging with people outside our church buildings. That many people will not come to our church buildings was demonstrated in recent research conducted by Brierley Consultancy. The research reveals that midweek church activities and church-based community engagement in London churches only affects a little more than 10% of London's population.[35] This means that about 90% of London's population is unreached by our church activities and is why the efforts of Lincoln and Akosua in the first example and those of RCCG in the second are commendable, as they begin to recognise the limitations of the attractional model of church. This change in reflection and practice demonstrates that BMC are developing missional strategies that possibly will break the barriers of being

---

partnership with 3D Ministries based in Sheffield. I was part of some of these conversations.

[35] 'What the London Census Reveals: London's Churches are Growing', June 2013. Available at http://www.brierleyconsultancy.com/images/londonchurches.pdf (accessed 7th August 2014).

mono-ethnic churches. However, it is important to remember from the discussion in chapter one that not all BMC are mono-ethnic churches.

A kingdom theology: the case of Jonathan Oloyede

A third response to mono-ethnic mission strategies is the development of a kingdom theology that understands that God's kingdom is bigger than our church tradition, nationality or postcode. One African church leader who has developed this theme consistently and embodies it is Jonathan Oloyede, the convener of the UK National Day of Prayer. His drive for a kingdom theology that brings unity in diversity reflects and further builds on Philip Mohabir's vision when ACEA was set up in the 1980s. Jonathan arrived in the UK from Nigeria in 1991 with the intention of visiting and spending time with his family. However, when he arrived, God spoke these words to him: 'Jonathan, you are not here by accident; you are here by divine design. You are here as part of My recruitment to this part of the world in preparation for the coming of My Son, Jesus. Drop your agenda therefore and pick up My programme.'

Jonathan later reflected, 'It was so clear and scary, so much so that I thought Jesus was coming back in 1994!'[36] Jonathan was involved in a church plant in East London which led to the founding of Glory House in Plaistow. However, his vision of seeing different nationalities working together in partnership for the sake of God's kingdom led to the founding of Global Day of Prayer, now National Day of Prayer (NDOP) in the UK. National Day of Prayer attracts Christians from different nationalities, cultures and church traditions. The vision for prayer and unity has also seen Jonathan working in partnership with organisations such as the Evangelical Alliance, Soul Survivor, Tearfund and New Wine.

---

[36] Olofinjana, *Turning the Tables on Mission*, p.97.

Intercultural theology: African pastors leading White Majority Churches and multicultural churches

Jonathan helped developed a kingdom theology through the NDOP movement. How are other African and Caribbean pastors and missionaries developing this? Some are doing it through engaging and interacting with other cultures through the matrix of the multicultural church context.

I was sent by my Pentecostal church in Nigeria in 2004 to plant a church here in the UK. However, I decided not to plant that church because I did not want to lead a Nigerian church. After observing few Nigerian churches in the UK and how they were struggling to reach the indigenes, I decided to join a British Historic Church. I started attending a Baptist church in South East London because I wanted to understand the church culture and context in the UK. This Baptist church was a multicultural church and became the place where I learnt the dynamics and challenges of a multicultural church setting.

After serving as a youth leader and student minister in the church for a while, I became one of the pastors of the church (serving alongside a white female clergy), making me the first black minister in the 100 years of the church's history. Since then, I have had the privilege of leading a White Majority Church and am currently leading Woolwich Central Baptist Church, a multicultural, multi-ethnic, intergenerational church in South East London. I am convinced, from my experience and theological reflection, that multicultural churches are a sign of God's kingdom on earth and that they signify a new way of expressing humanity. This is what Bruce Milne refers to in his book, *Dynamic Diversity*, as the 'New Humanity Church': a new kind of community of God's people that transcends any form of division.[37]

---

[37] Bruce Milne, *Dynamic Diversity: The New Humanity Church for Today and Tomorrow* (Nottingham: Inter-Varsity Press, 2006), pp.15-16.

A further significant factor in the discourse on reverse mission is that some British churches invited ministers to come and lead their church or to be part of the leadership team. This marks another theological shift, because Britain is not only now a mission field, as recognised by Philip Mohabir in the 1950s, but also now recognises that pastors and missionaries from the Majority World can help and contribute to God's mission. In a recent book of survey analysis by the Evangelical Alliance, it was revealed that 74% of Christians in the UK believe that Britain now needs missionaries.[38] In recognition of this, Peter Oyugi was invited in 2005 by Elmfield Church in North West London to be their lead pastor.[39] Elmfield Church is an independent evangelical church with Brethren roots. One of the reasons the leadership invited Peter was to help the church reflect more of the cultural diversity of the local area; it was previously a white majority, upper middle-class congregation.[40]

BMC and community and social engagement

A further development within the theology of BMC is community and social engagement. It appears that once upon a time BMC were so conscious of heaven that they were of no earthly relevance. Les Isaac, reflecting on this, observed that BMC in the 1970s were introverted institutions that were holding

---

[38] William Ackah, 'Evangelicals and their Global Connections', in Greg Smith (ed), *21st Century Evangelicals: Reflections on Research by the Evangelical Alliance* (Watford: Instant Apostle, 2015), p.164.

[39] Olofinjana, *Turning the Tables on Mission*, p.150.

[40] Olofinjana, *Turning the Tables on Mission*, p.152. Peter is currently working with African Inland Mission (AIM) as a mobiliser for the South of England and Wales and one of the directors of Centre for Missionaries from the Majority World.

the fort until Christ comes again.[41] A heaven-bound doctrine is perhaps one way BMC coped with their exclusion from British churches and society in the 1960s and 1970s. A consequence was social action projects such as the Pentecostal Credit Union (PCU) for their own members. To an outsider, such works would appear irrelevant to the wider community, but to insiders it was recognised that they were meeting needs that would not be met elsewhere. This, combined with the traditional understanding of mission as primarily evangelism, led many BMC to see social and community engagement as secondary or irrelevant. BMC are very good at evangelism – that is, proclaiming the gospel – but relatively poor at social action initiatives that demonstrate care for the community.

The story is changing, however, as many BMC are now leading community projects and initiatives such as operating food banks, becoming CAP centres,[42] running winter night shelters, and offering debt counselling, immigration services and employment training. This change is reflected in my definition of reverse mission as holistic mission.

A significant social and community engagement project that has emerged from within the BMC is the Street Pastors initiative. In response to the rise of gun and knife crime and a rereading of the story of the Good Samaritan in the light of urban crisis (Luke 10:25-37), the Street Pastors initiative was birthed in 2003 by Rev Les Isaac and Rev David Shosanya.

Street Pastors is an attempt to demonstrate the practical love of God on the streets at night. It has now become a recognised initiative in the UK and other parts of the world. A significant

---

[41] Les Isaac, 'Social Issues and the Black Church' in Joe Aldred and Keno Ogbo (eds), *The Black Church in the 21st Century* (London: Darton, Longman & Todd, 2010), p.104.
[42] Christians Against Poverty (CAP) is a Christian charity helping to alleviate causes of poverty in the UK such as debt, addiction and unemployment.

element of Street Pastors is that it brings together Christians from different traditions and allows the church to work together with the police and local authorities. The church's partnership with the police and local government to support each other in order to benefit the community is known in the Street Pastors' training as the 'urban trinity'.[43] For example, in the Royal Borough of Greenwich, Street Pastors have managed to establish a good working relationship with the local authorities and the police. This is expressed in a jointly organised annual carol service, which is well attended by the local community. This is a celebration of the working-out of the concept of urban trinity!

Healing, deliverance and *missio Dei* (God's mission)

Having considered the various efforts of some BMC to develop multicultural mission strategies and their social and community activism, another aspect of their mission that also needs to be considered is healing and deliverance. This is one of the significant missiological contributions of BMC to the theology of mission. However, I am not implying that they have a monopoly on this ministry because there are British evangelicals and charismatics who also engage in healing and deliverance.

The belief that the supernatural world is real and affects the natural world is very strong within BMC. The supernatural world is perceived as a world of spirits, both good and evil. African and Caribbean world-view and culture is very religious, and this affects every sphere of life. Therefore there is no sacred and secular divide within African and Caribbean religion and culture.

Another implication of this religious world-view is that it understands that some problems or issues have a spiritual cause and can therefore be solved by a spiritual solution. For example,

---

[43] Les Isaac and Rosaline Davies, *Street Pastors* (Eastbourne: David C. Cook, 2009), p.117.

if someone is ill, one understanding is that there is a spiritual force behind the illness or sickness. This is why within the African Traditional Religion people will consult the witch doctor or herbalist whenever they have a problem. The African and Caribbean view of the relationship between the supernatural and natural worlds, where spirits can affect the natural world, is similar to the world-view that was prevalent at the time of Jesus. This is why Jesus engaged in healing and deliverance (Acts 10:38).

Jesus preached, taught, fed the poor and healed people (Matthew 9:35-38). The Nazareth manifesto (Luke 4:18-19), a key text used to describe the engagement of the church in socio-economic and political issues, can also be interpreted as valid for healing ministry. A reading in context of that passage reveals that Jesus engaged in casting out demons and healing people after reading that text (Luke 4:31-41). If Jesus' mission involved casting out demons and healing the sick, then it begs the question why most of our conversations on the *missio Dei* ignore or don't emphasise this aspect of His mission? It appears that we have what I refer to as a selective hermeneutic, where we emphasise certain elements of Jesus' mission, such as feeding the poor, but ignore His casting out demons. God's mission cannot be reduced to only social action because Jesus engaged in healing ministry as a sign of God's kingdom on earth (Matthew 11:1-6). It is therefore imperative that in participating in God's mission, we have to engage in healing and deliverance ministries.

BMC are very good at exercising this aspect of God's mission by setting people free from demonic oppression and illnesses. This is enforcing God's kingdom on earth in dark places and spaces where the enemy wants to rule. *Missio Dei* is about proclaiming God's kingdom, whether in the physical by liberating people from unjust structures and oppression, or in the spiritual by healing the sick and casting out demons. This is the New Testament model of mission, and the one that the apostles were faithful in exercising (Acts 2:42-47; Acts 3:1-10; 16:16-18).

It must be acknowledged, however, that there have been some bad practices of deliverance, where some BMC rogue pastors have accused children of having witchcraft spirits and their efforts to exorcise have amounted to abuse. This abuse, along with the deaths of Victoria Climbié in 2000 and Kristy Bamu in 2012 based on witchcraft allegations, has led to serious concerns by the British public as well as within the BMC community. BMC leaders exercising the ministry of healing must be very careful to follow Jesus' model in the New Testament as opposed to misplaced cultural practices that have no basis in Scripture. Jesus never accused children of witchcraft spirits; rather He welcomed them (Mark 10:13-16). Pastors and churches have a duty and responsibility to safeguard children from abusive practices.

These incidents of alleged witchcraft accusations have led to media stereotypes of BMC. This in turn has led to public perception of BMC as criminal churches that need to be ostracised. The demonised public image of the BMC by the media has been challenged by BMC leaders. An example was a joint press release in 2010 by the Evangelical Alliance and Churches Together in England (CTE) in response to the Channel 4 TV documentary *Dispatches*, which implied that some BMC were involved in child abuse cases related to witchcraft. Dr Joe Aldred, then secretary of Minority Ethnic Christian Affairs for CTE, said this in the statement:

> Churches providing social and spiritual support in the African and Caribbean communities in the UK have a long history of exemplary work that has been recognised widely.
> This Christian community has never encouraged or tolerated abuses of children and vulnerable people. This remains the case and anyone found breaking the

law under the guise of faith should be reported to the authorities.

None of the churches or pastors featured in the programme are members of the Evangelical Alliance or Churches Together in England.[44]

Emerging African theologians and the development of theology of mission in Britain

Black British theology has been developed since the 1990s, particularly by Caribbean scholars such as Robert Beckford and Anthony Reddie. However, one of the current developments that needs to be discussed in this chapter is the rise of African theologians who are charting emergent mission theology in the British context. As I continued to reflect on the nature and development of African Christianity in Britain, I began to ask myself this question: Now that we have thousands of African churches in Britain, who are the theologians reflecting, critiquing and most importantly writing about with regard to African Christianity in Britain? In essence, who are the theologians of the African Church Movement in Britain?

This is not an easy question to answer because, although we have many African pastors with Master's degrees and doctorates in theology, very few African pastors are writing. Perhaps I should say that they are not writing theological textbooks, because there are many African pastors writing motivational and inspirational books to encourage and enable believers to deal with the issues they face in everyday life. So why are African pastors not writing theological textbooks, or books that

---

[44] Joint press release statement from the Evangelical Alliance, Churches Together in England and the Churches Child Protection Advisory Service in response to the *Dispatches* programme 'Britain's Witch Children', 28th July 2010.

demonstrate that they are reflecting on their history, church and mission?

The first reason is the perception that studying theology is either not relevant or might even lead to one losing his or her faith. Some have experienced theological institutions and felt that some of their studies were impractical and irrelevant. Some African pastors and lay leaders who have studied theology at one of the British theological institutions mentioned to me that if they were to preach the way they were taught to preach, no one from their congregation would return the following Sunday! This sounds shocking, but what they were alluding to was the issue of being taught by someone highly qualified in systematic theology and hermeneutics but who, it was felt, lacked pastoral and ministerial experience. Added to this is unawareness of the dynamics and context of ministry in a BMC.

Is this opinion justified? On the one hand, we need more African pastors and lay leaders to have theological and ministerial training so as to be prepared to minister in a postmodern British society, but on the other hand we also need theological tutors who have current and relevant pastoral and ministerial experience in order to combine head and heart in a theological classroom. Having theological tutors whose pastoral and ministry experience were in the 1960s and 1970s is not good enough! In addition, we need more than just white British theological educators in our theological institutions because the face of the church in Britain is now multi-ethnic.

A second reason why I think African pastors are not writing theological textbooks is the nature of the traditional academic publishing system. Academic publishing is based on academic qualifications or being attached to a theological institution or centre. This means that if you do not have a chair in a theological institution or are not at least attached to a college or a university, your work is not likely to be considered. For traditional academic publishing, it appears that it is necessary to know well-known

Christians or to have a good reference from someone inside the publishing house. This is partly why some African pastors and churches have established their own publishing companies to print their inspirational self-help books.

The third and final reason is the practical need, which many African pastors have adopted. African pastors seem to prefer to write about how to solve issues such as their congregation's financial problems rather than about the history of African Pentecostal churches in Britain. This is partly driven by the needs in some of these churches, which range from immigration issues, visa restrictions, marital problems and financial problems. But it has to be said that while many of these motivational books are written with the practical and urgent needs of people in mind, others are done by pastors who have their own agenda of preaching the Prosperity Gospel. The more books you write on success, the more people buy them, the more money you make! African pastors must take the time to reflect on the nature of our churches, doctrines and practices, and write to help educate and disciple their followers.

Having considered some reasons why African pastors are not writing theological textbooks, it is important to mention a few in Britain who are writing and reflecting on the African church movement as it is unfolding. This is not an exhaustive list, but here are some examples.

Dr Afe Adogame is possibly one of the best-known African scholars, not only in Britain but also in Europe, North America and Africa. He has written, contributed to and edited more books and articles than any other African scholar I am aware of in Britain. His bibliography is impressive: he has authored more than ten books and written countless articles in edited books and academic journals on African Christianity in diaspora. Afe is

Lecturer in World Christianity and Religious Studies at the University of Edinburgh.[45]

Rev Dr Kate Coleman is a Baptist minister and theologian who is actively involved in developing strategic leaders. She is a womanist theologian who reflects on the issues that affect women in leadership, with a particular focus on black women in leadership. She is the author of *7 Deadly Sins of Women in Leadership*[46] and has contributed to academic journals and books. Kate also teaches at various theological institutions, one of which is Cliff College. Kate is the Director of Next Leadership, a cutting-edge organisation that is involved in training and equipping leaders.

Rev Dr Chigor Chike is an ordained Anglican minister in East London and has written three books on African Christianity in Britain. The first is *African Christianity in Britain*.[47] This book surveyed the doctrines and practices of African Christians in Britain. The second, *Voices from Slavery: Life and Beliefs of African Slaves in Britain*,[48] considers the life of four African Christian slaves in Britain and draws on their theological significance. His most recent work is *Holy Spirit in African Christianity: An Empirical Study*.[49] This research work is based on his PhD thesis

---

[45] The University of Edinburgh staff profiles. Available at http://www.ed.ac.uk/schools-departments/global-development/about/staff/afe-adogame (accessed 20th July 2015).

[46] Kate Coleman, *7 Deadly Sins of Women in Leadership* (Birmingham: Next Leadership Publishing, 2010).

[47] Chigor Chike, *African Christianity in Britain* (Milton Keynes: Author House, 2007).

[48] Chigor Chike, *Voices from Slavery: Life and Beliefs of African Slaves in Britain* (Milton Keynes: Author House, 2007).

[49] Chigor Chike, *Holy Spirit in African Christianity: An Empirical Study* (Milton Keynes: Authentic Media, 2015).

exploring the pneumatology (belief in the person and work of the Holy Spirit) of African Pentecostal churches and African Christians within Historic Churches in Britain.

Rev Joe Kapolyo is a Baptist minister and scholar whose academic credentials combine theology and social anthropology. Joe has experience of leading theological institutions in Africa and Britain. He has also worked with a number of mission organisations such as the Church Mission Society (CMS) and the Baptist Missionary Society (BMS). Joe has written books and has contributed book chapters as well as journal articles. He was one of the contributors to the *African Bible Commentary*[50] and the *Dictionary of Mission Theology*.[51]

Dr Babatunde Adedibu is one of the emerging African missiologists in Britain. Babatunde has written two books to date and has contributed to academic journals and books. His two books are *Storytelling: An Effective Communication Appeal in Preaching*[52] and *Coat of Many Colours*.[53] *Coat of Many Colours* documents the history, mission and theology of BMC. Babatunde is a Visiting Lecturer and Honorary Research Fellow at the University of Roehampton.

Dr Harvey Kwiyani is an African missiologist in Britain who has experience of the missional church conversation in North America and Britain. This experience is reflected in his new

---

[50] Tokunboh Adeyemo (ed), *African Bible Commentary* (Grand Rapids, MI: Zondervan Publishing, 2006).
[51] John Corrie (ed), *Dictionary of Mission Theology: Evangelical Foundations* (Nottingham: Inter-Varsity Press, 2007).
[52] Babatunde Adedibu, *Storytelling: An Effective Communication Appeal in Preaching* (London: Wisdom Summit, 2009).
[53] Babatunde Adedibu, *Coat of Many Colours* (London: Wisdom Summit, 2012).

book, *Sent Forth: African Missionary Work in the West.*[54] This book, which builds on earlier scholarship, brings us up to date with the African missionary movement in the West. The strength of the book lies in the fact that it attempts to view in holistic terms the missionary work of Africans in the West and the missional church conversation as it is unfolding. Harvey is the founding director of Missio Africanus, an initiative designed to help the missionary work of Africans in Britain.[55] This is achieved through the Missio Africanus conference and journal. The initiative is supported by the Church Mission Society, Birmingham Christian College, the Centre for Missionaries from the Majority World and RCCG – Open Heavens London. Harvey teaches missions, leadership, and African studies at Birmingham Christian College and at CMS in Oxford. He is also a Research Fellow at the Cuddesdon Study Centre at Ripon College, Cuddesdon.

Israel Olofinjana: I feel it is appropriate to include my name as I have done a fair amount of writing and reflection on African Christianity, history and mission in Africa and Britain. I have written three books: *Reverse in Ministry and Missions: Africans in the Dark Continent of Europe,*[56] *20 Pentecostal Pioneers in Nigeria,*[57] and *Turning the Tables on Mission: Stories of Christians from the Global South in Britain.*[58] I have also contributed chapters to

---

[54] Harvey Kwiyani, *Sent Forth: African Missionary Work in the West* (New York: Orbis Books, 2014).

[55] See http://missioafricanus.org/t/ (accessed 1st April 2015).

[56] Israel Olofinjana, *Reverse in Ministry and Missions: Africans in the Dark Continent of Europe* (Milton Keynes: Author House, 2010).

[57] Israel Olofinjana, *20 Pentecostal Pioneers in Nigeria* (Bloomington, IN: Xlibiris, 2011).

[58] Israel Olofinjana (ed), *Turning the Tables on Mission: Stories of Christians from the Global South in Britain* (Watford: Instant Apostle, 2013).

academic textbooks and written journal articles. In addition, I am one of the directors of the Centre for Missionaries from the Majority World, an initiative established to train and equip missionaries and pastors from Africa, Asia, Latin America and the Caribbean.[59]

While I have only focused in this section on African pastors and scholars writing in Britain, it is necessary to mention that there are others who have reflected and written about African Christianity, churches in Britain and BMC in general. These are, among many others:

- Dr Robert Beckford, the leading black theologian in Britain

- Dr Anthony Reddie, another leading black theologian in Britain

- Dr Joe Aldred, Pentecostal and Multicultural Relations, CTE

- Mark Sturge, author of *Look What the Lord has Done*

- Dr David Muir, co-chair of the National Church Leaders Forum and Lecturer in Ministerial Theology at the University of Roehampton

- Dr Richard Burgess, Lecturer in Ministerial Theology at the University of Roehampton

- Rev Dr Michael Jagessar, theologian and former Moderator of the United Reformed Church (URC)[60]

---

[59] See http://www.cmmw.co.uk/ (accessed 1st April 2015).
[60] This section was first published on my blog on 8th January 2015 as 'Emerging African Theologians in Britain'. It has been adapted for this book. See https://israelolofinjana.wordpress.com/2015/01/08/emerging-african-theologians-in-britain/ (accessed 17th March 2015).

Towards structural change in society

BMC have come a long way since their inception in the 1930s. Some have grown from being rejected migrant sanctuaries to building multicultural and multi-ethnic churches that are engaging with the community. In addition, some BMC are articulating a theology of reverse mission that sees the UK as a mission field, and we are also beginning to see the emergence of BMC theologians. While all of this is commendable, BMC must further develop their mission theology in order to move from the provision of social services to the transformation of society.

Reverse mission cannot remain at evangelism, church planting, healing and social and community engagement; it has to address issues of structure that will bring lasting socio-economic and political change to society. This will mean shifting from just providing social services, which BMC do very well, to bringing changes that affect structures and institutions. Examples of these systemic and structural issues include fighting institutional racism, tackling unemployment, poverty reduction, tackling under-achievement in education, inequalities in the health system, immigration policies and system, and the prison system. These are issues that affect three categories of people, although not exclusively: migrants, deprived ethnic communities and the white working classes.

Some BMC leaders are already engaging with some of these issues through various agencies. In this respect, it is worth mentioning the following leaders:

- Nims Obunge, founder of Peace Alliance

- Celia Apeagyei-Collins, founder of Rehoboth Foundation

- Les Isaac, founder of Street Pastors

- Jonathan Oloyede, convener of NDOP UK

- Dionne Gravesande, head of Churches Christian Aid

- Agu Irukwu, Senior Pastor of Jesus House, RCCG

- Joe Aldred, Pentecostal and Multicultural Relations of Churches Together in England

- Donnett Thomas, Chair of Churches Together in South London (CTSL)

- Joel Edwards, International Director of Micah Challenge

- David Muir, founder of Faith in Britain

- Ade Omooba, Director of Christian Concern for our Nation (CCFON)

- Kate Coleman, Director of Next Leadership

All of these leaders have made a conscious effort to influence change in society. However, we need a wider participation and consciousness if we are going to move from having influence to having impact. Joel Edwards has observed:

> Impact goes beyond influence. I don't really care where you come from in the missionary enterprise, structural change is part and parcel of that mission, and that is a part of the challenge facing those of us from ethnic minorities. And I think this is about dialogue and partnership.[61]

How can we affect systemic and structural change?

First, we have to develop a theology of mission that has transformation of society at the heart of its agenda. The previous section discussed current developments and the efforts of African pastors and scholars in charting new mission theology. However, this is still in its early stages and a work in progress.

---

[61] Olofinjana, *Turning the Tables on Mission*, p.220.

Part of the development of a theology of mission seeking to transform society will mean BMC, and in particular African Pentecostal churches, engaging with black British theology. In addition, it will mean more pastors and church leaders undergoing theological training to postgraduate degree level so as to be equipped to reflect theologically on mission and engage differently. To develop this mission theology or engage current contextual theologies, scholars and practitioners will need to work together. The dichotomy that often exists between scholars and practitioners of any church persuasion will have to be bridged in order to construct a theology that will affect structures. The National Church Leaders Forum (NCLF) appears to be doing this at the moment by bringing together black British theologians, activists and BMC leaders in order to educate and mobilise BMC for political action.

An important question to ask at this stage is: can Prosperity Gospel be constructed as a viable holistic mission theology that can transform society? I will return to this shortly.

Secondly, BMC need to develop a prophetic and radical voice that is able to speak out against unjust structures and advocate on behalf of the poor. We must be like Moses, who was able to speak to Pharaoh about the oppression and enslavement of the children of Israel. This means it will not be enough for pastors to be bold at the pulpit about God's holiness and power and not be bold about speaking out against injustice in the public square. It is not also enough to have Members of Parliament, politicians and people in power as friends and to shy away from raising justice issues with them. We must endeavour to speak truth to power, even if it will mean that we risk losing some friendships.

It is worth mentioning that NCLF,[62] in order to educate and mobilise the black church politically, has put together a Black

---

[62] NCLF is the authentic national voice of the black church in Britain seeking to represent BMC interests and concerns through representation, advocacy, political education and action and the

Church Political Manifesto. The strategy of this manifesto is to mobilise the African and Caribbean churches and the wider black community for social and political action. This is done through encouraging our churches to actively engage in socio-cultural, political and economic institutions locally and nationally. NCLF also hopes to strengthen communities and to promote active citizenship and the common good.[63] The political manifesto, a first of its kind, addresses nine topics:

- church and community
- policing and criminal justice
- prisons
- mental health
- voting and political mobilisation
- family and marriage
- youth and education
- media, music, arts and culture
- international aid and development

Each topic offers reflections on the current situation, the biblical picture and future recommendations. The manifesto was officially launched on 14th March 2015 at Deeper Life Bible Church building, Transformation House in Clapham Junction, London. The launch was attended by more than 200 people representing the different BMC, black activists, Members of Parliament and the general public. The manifesto was produced

media. It started in 2011 after the demise of ACEA. The steering group comprises church leaders, activists and theologians from the African and Caribbean Christian community.
[63] Dr David Muir and Pastor Ade Omooba, 'Black Church Political Mobilisation: A Manifesto for Action' (a document produced by NCLF), January 2015, p.3.

for the 2015 General Election to raise with major political parties and institutions the concerns of the BME community. Copies of the manifesto were sent to the Prime Minister David Cameron, the then Labour leader Ed Miliband, and all Members of Parliament.

Another example of BMC involvement in the political sphere is the government consultation and dialogue with BMC leaders on the Human Trafficking and Modern-day Slavery Bill. In a round-table meeting held on 10th March 2015, discussions were held concerning the Bill and support for victims of human trafficking. The discussion, jointly organised by Pentecostal and Multicultural Relations of Churches Together in England, the Human Trafficking Foundation and the Home Office, saw many BMC leaders and black activists in attendance. These examples of BMC political engagement are signs of movement in the right direction.

Thirdly, we need to encourage and empower more people in our congregations to become professionals such as doctors, lawyers, health workers, teachers, social workers, entrepreneurs, civil servants and politicians. Some BMC are very good at this and organise seminars and conferences that help and encourage people to fulfil their professional dreams and ambitions. In cases where these professionals are already in our churches, pastors and church leaders must encourage and educate them to engage with the socio-political issues that particularly affect immigrants, deprived ethnic communities and white working classes.

This is already happening in some BMC. An example is RCCG which encourages its members to become leaders in the areas of politics, business and the media. One of the RCCG congregations, Trinity Chapel in London, has this strapline as its vision: 'Developing Leaders: Influencing Society'. Also, Jesus House in North London, the flagship church of RCCG in the UK, launched in 2013 its new social enterprise, the Barnet Youth Business Incubator (BaYBI) to equip young people to start their own businesses. The project is run in partnership with the youth charity Elevation Networks and Barnet Council. The project supports around 100 young people between the ages of 16 and 24 who are interested in running their own business.[64]

Lastly, I want to emphasise that in order to change structures, we need to work together with other churches and agencies. We need to work in partnership with Historic Churches to effect this change and transformation in society. This partnership will mean more Christians from BMC constituencies occupying strategic leadership positions within the UK church structures, Bible colleges, mission organisations and para-church organisations. This is important in demonstrating equality and genuine partnership. Partnerships that are colonial and still see us as inferiors need to be challenged. This is why we need to engage with institutions, with the various para-church organisations and with denominational structures. I am aware this may mean that some of us might have to undertake postgraduate studies, but any meaningful partnership will have to see us as equals and not as subordinates.

How does this partnership look, and what is the history of BMC and Historic Churches working together? Before exploring these questions in the third chapter, I want to consider Prosperity Gospel as a possible holistic mission theology that can transform society.

Reconstruction of Prosperity Gospel as a holistic theology of mission

One of the points I raised above, concerning BMC tackling systemic and structural issues, is the development of a mission

---

[64] 'Church Raising New Generation of Entrepreneurs', *Christian Today*, February 2013. Available at http://www.christiantoday.co.uk/article/church.raising.new.generatio n.of.entrepreneurs/31645.htm (accessed 15th February 2013).

theology that has transformation of society at the heart of its agenda. What I want to explore in this section is whether the Prosperity preaching of some BMC can be contextualised and reconstructed so that instead of its current individualistic consumeristic approach it becomes a vehicle for structural change. In order to do this, and as mentioned above, we must firstly recognise that there is a thriving black British theology community in the UK, but it appears that it is distanced from some BMC because of differences of purpose and approach.

While the work of NCLF is bridging this gap, the major differences can be seen in the point of departure: while black theology emphasises the black experience, BMC place their emphasis on the Scriptures as God's Word. The agenda of black theology is to see the liberation of black people from oppressive and unjust structures that marginalise. It also seeks to advocate for the black community economically, politically and socially. On the other hand, the agenda of BMC is to do mission through evangelism, church planting, and social and community engagement, as previously discussed.

While these purposes are not opposed to each other (on the contrary, they complement each other), it seems there is tension between the exponents. One possible reason for this is that some BMC in Britain do not have a sense of ownership of black British theology – or, to put it another way, they are not involved in the formation processes of such theology. It must be clarified, however, that some of the Caribbean Pentecostal churches that started around the 1940s to the 1960s, and some of the BMC within Historic Churches, are engaging with black British theology. It appears to be African Pentecostal Churches that have distanced themselves.[65]

---

[65] Drew Smith, William Ackah and Anthony Reddie (eds), *Churches, Blackness and Contested Multiculturalism* (New York: Palgrave Macmillan), pp.15-16.

One way forward for BMC to own a theology is to bridge the gap between black British theologians and BMC leaders in order to encourage dialogue. BMC can greatly benefit from the work of black British theologians such as Dr Anthony Reddie, who has developed black theology as an empowering educational tool; Dr Robert Beckford who is articulating a black political Pentecostal theology (the Dread Thesis);[66] Dr Joe Aldred's Theology of Respect which brings an ecumenist perspective to the scene;[67] and Dr David Muir's Theology of Ascent which asserts that black theology must move away from an oppression/liberation dialectic to one of personal acceptance and affirmation of radical equality in God.[68] As seen from the example of NCLF, the gap between black British theologians and BMC leaders is already closing.

A further development that has to be noticed and taken seriously in the construction of a mission theology for BMC in the UK is Prosperity Gospel. What is meant by the term 'Prosperity Gospel'? Is it another gospel? Prosperity is considered to be part of the gospel, because it is conceived as the good news of redemption lift to those who have experienced suffering and tasted extreme poverty. This redemption lift is a holistic mission in that it asserts forgiveness of sins, education for the mind, deliverance from spiritual forces, health for the weak and material blessings for the poor.[69]

---

[66] Robert Beckford, *Jesus is Dread* (London, Darton, Longman & Todd Ltd, 1998) and *Dread and Pentecostalism* (London: SPCK, 2000).

[67] Aldred, *Respect*, pp.180-184.

[68] David Muir, 'Theology and the Black Church', *The Black Church in the 21st Century* (London: Darton, Longman & Todd Ltd, 2010), pp.23-24.

[69] Israel Olofinjana, 'Nigerian Pentecostals: Towards Consumerism or Prosperity?' in Afe Adogame (ed), *The Public Face of African New Religious Movements in Diaspora* (Surrey: Ashgate Publishing Limited, 2014), pp.233-234.

Many articles and books have been written by both black and white scholars critiquing and condemning the preaching of Prosperity messages and its abusive practices. This is justified because some Prosperity preachers have become wealthy through exploitation of the poor. There are Pentecostal preachers, black and white, who have bought private jets, luxurious cars and expensive mansions through church funds donated by the poor. Western capitalism, manifested through consumerism, materialism and individualism, can be argued to be at the heart of Prosperity preaching; therefore it begs the question whether it can be reconstructed as a mission theology to tackle unjust structures and transform society.

Without condoning or excusing the greed of the perpetuators who use Prosperity preaching to abuse the poor, I think there is an element in Prosperity Gospel that can be reconstructed positively. There are theologians such as Dr Dwight Hopkins, Dr Robert Beckford, Dr Amos Yong, Dr Gideon Byamugisha, Dr Shayne Lee and Dr Lois Ann Lorentzen, among others, who have articulated passionately about the positive contributions Prosperity preaching could bring.

Following the work of some of these pioneers, I have begun in some of my writings to reconstruct Prosperity Gospel on the British scene as a viable response to migrant needs.[70] In these writings I argue that Prosperity Gospel should be understood as a contextual theology responding to the socio-economic needs of migrant communities in Britain. A further reconstruction here will be to ask the following questions:

• Can Prosperity Gospel speak for the oppressed and marginalised?

---

[70] Olofinjana, *Reverse in Mission*, pp.54-55. Olofinjana, *Nigerian Pentecostals*, pp.233-254.

- Can the wealth generated from Prosperity Gospel be used to tackle the HIV/AIDS pandemic that is plaguing many African and Caribbean nations?

- Can it help to reduce poverty in Africa and be used as a viable alternative resource for economic development and empowerment in Africa and the Caribbean?

This will mean that BMC must move away from a Prosperity message that is self-centred and individualistic towards a more robust one that articulates blessings for the community. At present, many Prosperity preachers seem to encourage their church members to prosper in all areas of life. But after prospering, what comes next? This question is not often asked, which is why so many people prosper only for themselves. This is why the Prosperity message can be self-centred and inward looking.

What would happen if Prosperity preachers were to start articulating that the reason God prospers people, or will prosper them, is so that they can be a blessing to their community? I have definitely heard this version of Prosperity preached before, but the problem is that it is not a popular version. This type of Prosperity message would aim to be a blessing to the community by advocating for marginalised people, empowering and resourcing the poor. This version can be appropriately referred to as 'Commonwealth Gospel',[71] because the wealth would be common and not individualistic. In addition, it would consider political freedom and socio-economic development of the oppressed as part of prospering. In other words, at its heart will be the Prosperity of the community in political and socio-economic terms. While Commonwealth Gospel would be politically conscious, it would not reduce salvation to only

[71] Robert Beckford, *Jesus Dub: Theology, Music and Social Change* (London: Routledge, 2006), pp.140-141.

political and economic freedom (a mistake often made by black and liberation theologies). It would rather be holistic in that making disciples, church planting, healing and social engagement would still be considered to be important gospel imperatives.

This truer version of Prosperity Gospel would see the success of individuals as a means to an end and not an end in itself. That is, prospering would lead to helping the less privileged and serving the poor. BMC would buy into the biblical vision of a communal Prosperity, as practised in the Acts of the Apostles (see Acts 2:44-47; 4:32-37). Trinitarian theology would also become useful in this process because the Godhead shares life and function in a communal understanding. The Triune God shared life with humanity through the incarnation of Jesus, meaning that the Godhead is not selfish.

This is not an intellectual dogma but rather a practical one that has implications for how the church shares its resources to benefit its community and the wider society.[72] The communal nature of the Godhead and the community dynamics of the New Testament church are similar to the community spirit that is rooted into the fabric of African and Caribbean societies, and this should be annexed for the welfare of humanity. In essence, the biblical paradigm where the community comes before individuals is resonant with African and Caribbean solidarity concepts. An example of this is the Ubuntu philosophy, as used and expressed in Southern Africa to define humanity's togetherness as opposed to individualistic views of human existence. Bishop Desmond Tutu, a key advocate of Ubuntu, defines it as:

---

[72] John Parratt, *Reinventing Christianity: African Theology Today* (Cambridge: William B. Eerdmans Publishing Company, and Trenton, NJ: African World Press Inc, 1995), pp.147-148.

My humanity being caught up, is inextricably bound up to, in theirs. We belong in a bundle of life. We say, 'a person is a person through other people.' It is not 'I think therefore I am.' It says rather: 'I am human because I belong.' I participate, I share.[73]

This notion of 'I am because you are' challenges the self-centredness of Prosperity Gospel and can possibly move it towards a shared community that privileges the community over the prospering of an individual. One mission practitioner who has begun to use Ubuntu to construct a mission theology for BMC is Rev David Shosanya, Regional Minister of Mission for the London Baptist Association (LBA). In a recent theology symposium organised by the Cinnamon Network, David articulated that the social action of African and Caribbean Pentecostal churches is not a response to the in-vogue concept of social action in the Western world, but rather that Ubuntu provides a historically and culturally relevant construct for the social action of BMC.[74] By this, David meant that the social action of BMC is unconsciously motivated by the world-view of Ubuntu which has historically and culturally conditioned and shaped who we are and what we do. He went on to highlight the Street Pastors initiative, which he co-founded with Rev Les Isaac, as an example of this paradigm, and explained that the reason it started was as a response to understanding this concept of humanity.

David's insight and combination of how Ubuntu subconsciously informs the Street Pastors initiative is a very

---

[73] Desmond Tutu, *No Future without Forgiveness* (London: Random House, 1999), p.35.
[74] David Shosanya presented a paper titled, 'The Gospel, Social Action and Community Engagement from a Pentecostal Perspective' at the Cinnamon Theology Symposium held at Emmanuel Centre, Marsham Street, London on 12th February 2015. I was in attendance.

powerful one and thus causes me to ask whether Ubuntu as an authentic African and Caribbean world-view can be regained to help reconstruct the Prosperity preaching of BMC? I use the word 'regained' because the excesses and abuses of Prosperity are evidence that this communal philosophy has been lost. If this communal world-view is regained and annexed by BMC preaching Prosperity, this will reinvigorate our mission and give hope to humanity.

The reshaping of Prosperity by Ubuntu ideology would mean that Commonwealth Gospel would give hope to the community, and it could change the image of black British theology from that of constant struggle and fight to that of a secure and mature identity. In other words, Commonwealth Gospel (a preferred term to Prosperity Gospel) will have an element of Respect and Ascent as expressed respectively by Joe Aldred and David Muir.

Prosperity Gospel must be considered by black British theologians as a contribution from some of the BMC because some of them identify with it; therefore it will be a good point of departure for any meaningful partnership. If this collaboration can be achieved, BMC will feel a sense of ownership of a theology, and black British theologians will be involved in critiquing it constructively. As mentioned, we are beginning to see signs of this collaboration through the work of NCLF, particularly through the production of the Black Church Political Manifesto mentioned earlier in this chapter.

Let us now return to what partnership looks like between BMC and Historic Churches, which is the subject of the next chapter.

Chapter three
Ecumenical partnerships between Historic Churches and BMC

A close examination of the history of the modern ecumenical movement since the inception of the World Council of Churches (WCC) in 1948 reveals that it has been initiated from a Western perspective. In some respects, it appears that Europeans and North Americans have the resources and personnel for mission and ecumenism and therefore Africans, Asians and Latin Americans can join in to fulfil God's mission on earth.

The Edinburgh missionary conference of 1910, which many see as the precursor of the modern ecumenical movement, was an example of this: of about 1,000 delegates, only a handful were from India, Japan and China, and there were none from Africa or South America. The centenary celebration of this event in Edinburgh in 2010 was significant, however, as Africans, Asians and Latin Americans took the lead in presenting theological papers from their various contexts. This mirrors the shift in world Christianity from North to South and the reverse flow of mission explored in the previous chapter. Despite this shift in mission, Western Christianity still has the resources and retains power with regard to ecumenical engagement, and this is reflected in the relationships between Historic Churches and the many BMC now flourishing in Britain. Some progress has been made between these churches, but there is still more work to be done.

There is a fresh expression of ecumenism emerging between Historic Churches and BMC. This is seen in cases of two churches sharing the same building, or three or four churches working together. The latter is mostly happening around mission and social action projects such as food banks, winter night shelters, Street Pastors initiatives and debt counselling courses. This type of grassroots intercultural ecumenism I have termed 'ecumenical partnerships', because the underlying principle (where it is working) is the affirmation of the equality of the churches involved. There is often still the problem of resources being in the hands of Historic Churches, because they have the majority of the buildings which some BMC rent and use.

What opportunities and challenges does this relationship through infrastructure constitute for BMC? This chapter considers examples of this intercultural ecumenism in London, some of the challenges involved, and ways to move towards an ecumenical partnership which affirms the equality of all. Particular attention is given to the history of ecumenism between BMC and Historic Churches.

Early cases of relationship between black and white Christians in Britain

I want to start my exploration by highlighting the fact that intercultural ecumenism is not a new thing and has some precedence in history. This can be found in the story of the Abolitionists. Olaudah Equiano (1745–1797), Quobna Ottobah Cugoano (1757–1790s) and Ignatius Sanchos (1729–1780) were all former African slaves who were involved in an ecumenical movement of Christians from various denominations rallying together to abolish the slave trade and work towards the resettlement of former slaves back to Sierra Leone.[75] This is a good example of missional intercultural ecumenism that leads to structural change in society.

---

[75] Chigor Chike, *Voices From Slavery* (Milton Keynes: Author House, 2007), pp.5-6.

Another example is the African American couple William and Ellen Craft and the Baptist minister Thomas L. Johnson (1836–1921). They all settled in Britain as missionaries and were part of the Foreign Anti-Slavery Society, an organisation founded to abolish slavery in the British Empire. They campaigned together actively against slavery and also preached against it in their sermons.[76]

Celestine Edwards (1858–1894) was born in Dominica but later settled in Edinburgh, Scotland. He joined the Temperance Movement, which advocated abstinence from alcohol. Celestine had a degree in theology and was a great public speaker; he spoke about human rights, denouncing racism and social Darwinism.[77] What is important here is that Celestine was part of an intellectual movement that worked towards a particular cause; in this case, helping people who had drinking problems.

Another example is the story of Harold Moody (already mentioned in chapter one), who became an active member of the London Missionary Society, a missionary movement seeking to reach out to people in different parts of the world. Moody later became the president of this society.

Daniels Ekarte (1890s–1964) was a Nigerian who founded African Churches Mission in Toxteth, Liverpool, in 1931. African Churches Mission had an ecumenical relationship with the Church of England and other churches, with the Bishop of Liverpool becoming the president of the mission and trustees being drawn from other church denominations. In addition, the Church of Scotland and the Catholic Church supported the mission financially. Interestingly, there is another church in Liverpool today led by a Nigerian, Temple of Praise Church, which works ecumenically with other churches. The founder of

---

[76] Jonathan Oloyede, 'Ecumenism and the Black Church', in Joe Aldred and Keno Ogbo (eds), *The Black Church in the 21st Century* (London: Darton, Longman & Todd Ltd, 2010), p.29.

[77] Sturge, *Look What the Lord has Done*, pp.71-72.

the church, Rev Dr Tani Omideyi, is also the ecumenical canon of the Liverpool Anglican Cathedral and a member of the Evangelical Alliance board.

These examples of missional intercultural ecumenism were rare for those periods and were not sustained. A new chapter in British church history emerged, as we have seen in chapter one, and this was the founding of BMC from the 1940s. As this has already been discussed I will not go into details here, but the period can be summarised as follows:

- 1940s–1960s: founding of the Caribbean Pentecostal and Holiness churches

- 1960s–1980s: founding of African Indigenous Churches (AIC)

- 1980s–present: founding of African and Caribbean New Pentecostal churches

- 1990s–present: founding of New-generation Caribbean churches

The reasons for the founding of BMC were also mentioned in the first chapter, but to summarise the main points:

- Missions and church plants to the UK

- Affiliation and loyalty to church brands

- Racism and social exclusion from British society

- Rejection by Historic Churches

- Perceived coldness of British Christianity – that is, a quiet reflective style of worship compared to the more expressive style in black Pentecostal churches

The neglect and rejection of black people, both by Historic Churches and by wider society, led to the founding of ecumenical bodies to represent the interests of BMC in the areas of training, ordination, social care, political advocacy, economic development and educational opportunities. To this end, the first ecumenical instrument, the International Ministerial Council of Great Britain (IMCGB) was founded in 1968 by the late Archbishop David Douglas and Archbishop Malachi Ramsay, who were both Caribbeans. IMCGB to some extent worked successfully with the British Council of Churches (BCC) and the government in representing the interests of BMC, but IMCGB was limited because it did not have the support of the wider leadership of BMC.[78] IMCGB still exists and is currently led by an apostolic team comprising Rt Rev Onye Obika, Rt Rev Sheila Douglas and Rt Rev Colin Mahoney.

Another organisation was founded in 1976: the Afro West Indian United Council of Churches (AWUCOC). AWUCOC enjoyed widespread support among the BMC leadership and was identified as the most authentic black Christian voice in the UK at that time. It also worked with the Home Office and the British Council of Churches representing the interests and issues facing BMC. BMC leaders from various Pentecostal and Holiness traditions played key roles in AWUCOC's development. Some of the leaders who were involved included the then overseer of New Testament Church of God, the late Rev Oliver Lyseight; the late Rev Desmond Pemberton from Wesleyan Holiness Church; the late Rev Dr I. O. Smith, the late Bishop Donald Bernard and Bishop Melvin Powell, all from New Testament Assembly; Archbishop Malachi Ramsay, founder of Shiloh United Church of Christ Apostolic Worldwide; and the late Dr Aston Gibson.

The BCC did not recognise some of the spiritual BMC, such as the Aladuras, as authentic or credible churches. The fact is that the BCC viewed many of the Caribbean and African Churches as sects, and this is reflected in Clifford Hill's publication, *Black*

---

[78] Sturge, *Look What the Lord has Done*, p.97.

Churches: West Indian and African Sects in Britain.[79] This, coupled with the fact that AWUCOC represented and appealed more to Caribbean churches than African churches, led to the establishment of the Council of African and Afro-Caribbean Churches (CAACC), founded by Father Olu Abiola, in 1979. CAACC represented the interests of Caribbean and African spiritual churches in the UK, such as the Aladuras from West Africa and Spiritual Baptists from Trinidad. This ecumenical agency continues today under the leadership of Father Olu Abiola.[80]

The Zebra Project

The Zebra Project was one of the first initiatives to attempt to bring together black and white churches. It was started in 1975 by Paul Charman and others as part of the Methodist Bow Project. The Zebra Project sought to develop relationships between the emerging BMC, mainly from a Caribbean background, and Historic Churches. It networked, hosted meetings and produced a number of publications. Its pioneering work led to it having a national profile, which was important in building relationships between Historic Churches and the emerging BMC. Part of its work was partnering with organisations such as the Conference for Christian Partnership (CCP), which provided a meeting place between the BCC and BMC and their organisations such as the AWUCOC and the CAACC. James Ashdown, who worked for the Project from 1987, has described the vision for the Project:

> The vision of the Zebra Project was of a church where people talk and share with each other in a frank and

---

[79] Clifford Hill, *Black Churches: West Indian and African Sects in Britain* (London, British Council of Churches, 1971).
[80] See http://www.caccorg.com/ (accessed 22nd January 2015).

open way for their mutual benefit. The Project attempted in multi-racial north and east London to discover ways of promoting this understanding, fellowship and common action. It arose out of a realisation that black and white Christians knew very little about each other, especially among congregations which were predominantly black or predominantly white membership. The aim was to encourage and facilitate face-to-face meetings. The Project has achieved the delicate balance of relationships between a large number of Christian groups.[81]

The Zebra Project was successful in that it managed to foster relationships between black and white church leaders. It also created local Zebra Projects in different parts of the country. Perhaps the most successful of its initiatives was the creation of the youth section, which facilitated relationships between black and white youth. Ashdown says of this:

Several local Zebra Project groups have sprung up. The first, which began as a minister's group, now has a youth section. Honesty, and a desire to face really deep issues, characterized this multi-racial and ecumenical group. It arose out of the concern about racial tensions in the local community and a realisation of the need for black and white ministers to get to know each other in order to respond to the needs of the community. As a development of local contacts in this area, a group of young people from a number of different denominations and racial backgrounds spent a few days together in a residential conference. The emphasis was on the contribution which can and should be made to our common society by different community groups.

---

[81] Questionnaire interview with James Ashdown on 5th November 2011, via email.

Other groups consisted mainly of lay Christians from individual congregations.

Below are the names of some of the church leaders who were involved in the Zebra Project. These leaders reflect the diversity, in terms of gender, church tradition and ethnicity, that the Zebra Project was able to pull together to work in unity:

- David Moore, then Methodist Superintendent of the Bow Mission

- Other Methodist ministers: Tony Holden, Arlington Trotman, Robin Milwood, Victor Watson and Paul Regan

- Father Abidoye, founding father of the Cherubim and Seraphim Church in Britain

- Father Olu Abiola, founder of Aladura International Church

- Ira Brooks, a New Testament Church of God minister

- Joel Edwards and Phyllis Thompson, other New Testament Church of God ministers

- I. O. Smith and Esme Beswick, New Testament Assembly ministers

- John Campbell, a United Reformed minister

- Myrna Lubin, a Catholic laywoman

- Gill Brewster (now Kanga) of the CANDL Project

The Zebra Project was disbanded in the early 1990s.

Conference for Christian Partnership and Centre for Black and White Christian Partnership

The work of the Conference for Christian Partnership (CCP) created a meeting space for black and white church leaders to meet and engage with one another. It also helped facilitate the sharing of church buildings between BMC and Historic

Churches. The CCP worked in partnership and supported the work of the Zebra Project. The CCP's work culminated in the establishment of the Centre for Black and White Christian Partnership.

Similar initiative to the Zebra Project was the Project in Partnership between Black and White, later renamed the Centre for Black and White Christian Partnership, which started in Birmingham in 1976. The first director of the Centre was the late German theologian, Dr Roswith Gerloff. She made significant contributions to the work of the Centre, and to black Christianity in Britain. This was particularly with regard to building relationships with leaders of BMC and documenting their history, mission and theology in her seminal work, *A Plea for British Black Theologies: The Black Church Movement in Britain in its Transatlantic Cultural and Theological Interaction with Oneness (Apostolic) and Sabbatarian Movements* (1992).

The co-chair of the Centre was father Olu Abiola, founder of Aladura International Church. He made significant contributions to the work of the Centre in the 1970s and 1980s, such as giving it direction and connecting Roswith Gerloff with leaders of various BMC.

The Centre's second director was the late Catholic theologian, Rev Dr Patrick Kalilombe, and the fourth and last was Dr Joe Aldred. The work of the Centre has now finished but appears to be continuing in a separate development with the founding of The Queens' Foundation for Ecumenical Theological Education.[82]

African and Caribbean Evangelical Alliance (ACEA)

The year 1984 marked a new interest in reconciliation between black and white churches and saw the launch of the West Indian

---

[82] For more information about Queen's, see http://www.queens.ac.uk/ (accessed 4th June 2015).

Evangelical Alliance (WIEA). The name changed in 1989 to the Afro-Caribbean Evangelical Alliance (ACEA) and finally to the African and Caribbean Evangelical Alliance (ACEA) in 1991 in recognition of African Christianity in Britain. ACEA worked in partnership with the Evangelical Alliance to foster partnership between BMC and the New Churches that had emerged from the Charismatic renewal in the 1970s. It also supported the development of unity among BMC (Africans and Caribbeans).

Philip Mohabir was a true pioneer in this initiative, as it was his vision that led to the founding of ACEA. As much as ACEA and the Evangelical Alliance tried to work together towards unity, there were still differences and divisions between BMC and British New Churches.[83] This was evident when Jonathan Oloyede attended an ACEA conference in Brighton in the year 2000 which was mainly attended by black people, and few white leaders. Four months later, Jonathan attended another conference in Cardiff, Wales, organised by the Evangelical Alliance, and to his surprise it was mainly white. Jonathan lamented to Joel Edwards (then Evangelical Alliance General Director) about the divide between black and white churches. Both Joel Edwards and Jonathan Oloyede outlined a course of action which began a journey of discovery into the depth and breadth of the chasm between the white and black Christian communities in the UK.[84]

---

[83] New Churches, sometimes called House Churches, are British evangelical churches which emerged through the Charismatic renewal in the 1960s and 1970s. Examples are Ichthus Christian Fellowship, Newfrontiers International, Covenant Ministries International, Cobham Christian Fellowship, Kingdom Faith Church, Cornerstone Christian Centre and many more.

[84] Jonathan Oloyede, 'Ecumenism and the Black Church' in Joe Aldred and Keno Ogbo (eds), *The Black Church in the 21st Century* (London: Darton, Longman & Todd Ltd, 2010), pp.30-31. Jonathan Oloyede, 'Techni-colour in Black and White', an unpublished paper.

Jonathan began to actively seek to engage and work together with white British evangelicals. One significant step was Glory House (Jonathan's former church) working together in mission with Soul Survivor, an evangelical church in North London through Soul in the City 2004. Jonathan also became involved in Spring Harvest (an evangelical festival in Britain). As mentioned in the previous chapter, Jonathan now leads Global Day of Prayer (GDOP) UK, which facilitates prayer for the British Isles, serving among different churches in the UK including BMC, Historic Churches and New Churches.

Jonathan Oloyede and Glory House also became involved in Transform Newham under the leadership of Rev Terry Diggines. Transform Newham is a model of how different churches can work together in fellowship and mission. It has also facilitated good working relationships between Historic Churches and BMC. Other good examples of this model in South East London are Southwark for Jesus chaired by Phil Stokes, Lewisham Churches United and Greenwich Church Leaders Forum. This new model of ecumenism is pioneering joint mission initiatives such as food banks, winter night shelters and Street Pastors.

In May 2011, owing to a lack of funds, ACEA officially closed. However, it appears that the work of ACEA has now continued in two distinct initiatives: the National Church Leadership Forum (NCLF) already mentioned in chapter two and the One People Commission.

National Church Leaders Forum

NCLF started in 2011 in an effort to bring greater cohesion and unity to the BMC.[85] To this end, a historic gathering of about 70 BMC leaders took place at KICC in Walthamstow, London. NCLF is organised by a steering group, with two co-chairs, Pastor Ade Omooba, co-founder of Christian Legal Centre (CLC)

---

[85] Muir and Omooba, 'Black Church Political Mobilisation', p.7.

and Christian Concern for our Nation (CCFON), and Dr David Muir, founder of Faith in Britain and Lecturer at the University of Roehampton. Other members of the steering group are key leaders from within the BMC constituency and include Dr Joe Aldred, secretary of Black and Multicultural Churches, CTE; Rev Celia Apeagyei-Collins, founder of Rehoboth Foundation; Dionne Gravesande, head of Churches for Christian Aid; Pastor Modupe Afolabi, Executive Administrator, RCCG, UK Central Office; Dr Michel Sacramento, head of African Francophone churches in the UK; and Pastor Tito Yisuku, Senior Pastor of Hope of Glory International Ministries.

NCLF is also supported by key church leaders, including:

- Pastor Matthew Ashimolowo, founder of KICC

- Rev Nezlin Sterling, former General Secretary of New Testament Assembly

- Rev Kingsley Appiagyei, founder of Trinity Baptist Church

- Pastor Kofi Banful, Senior Pastor of Praise Chapel

- Rev Esme Beswick, one of the senior leaders of the New Testament Assembly

- Bishop Eric Brown, Pentecostal President of CTE

- Bishop John Francis, founder of Ruach Church in Brixton

- Pastor Agu Irukwu, National Leader of RCCG UK

- Rev David Shosanya, LBA Regional Minister for Mission

- Bishop Wilton Powell, National Bishop of the Church of God of Prophecy

- Apostle Alfred Williams, founder of Christ Faith Tabernacle

- Pastor Michael Olawore, Senior Pastor of New Wine Church

One of the achievements of NCLF, as mentioned in the previous chapter, is the production of the first Black Church Political Manifesto which was used to engage the major political parties and MPs in the 2015 election. In addition, the Manifesto was used to educate and mobilise BMC concerning their voting rights and how to engage in politics, as it was sent to 3,000 churches. The Manifesto represents and clearly articulates the needs and aspirations of the BMC community. More work still needs to be done if the recommendations in the Manifesto are to be carried through. However, it is still too early to determine whether the Manifesto was a success and whether it has helped politicians understand the concerns of the BMC community.

The One People Commission

The second initiative, which seeks to work within the structures of the Evangelical Alliance to restructure it so that it becomes ethnically diverse, particularly in its leadership and governance, is the One People Commission, which started officially on 6th October 2011. The group is headed by Rev Yemi Adedeji, whose ecumenical credentials are substantial: he is an ordained Anglican clergyman as well as an ordained African Pentecostal minister.

The vision of the One People Commission is to see the UK church, in all its vibrant ethnic diversity, united as one. The One People Commission has gone a step further than ACEA in that while ACEA mainly focuses on African and Caribbean churches, the One People Commission has brought together leaders of white British, African, Caribbean, Asian and South American churches. This is done through gathering together for prayers, strategic planning and speaking into national issues on behalf of the UK church. One example of the latter was a video produced by the group to encourage Christians to vote in the 2015 General Election. The One People Commission includes key national church leaders such as:

- Rev Kingsley Appaigyei, Senior Pastor of Trinity Baptist Church

- Dr Daniel Chae, founder of Amnos Ministries

- Pastor Chrishanthy Sathiyaraj, Bethany Faith Ministries

- Bishop Eric Brown, Pentecostal President of CTE

- Pastor Celia Apeagyei-Collins, founder of Rehoboth Foundation

- Rev John Glass, General Superintendent of Elim Pentecostal Church

- Pastor Agu Irukwu, Chair of RCCG UK and Senior Pastor of Jesus House

- Dr Tani Omideyi, Senior Minister of Love and Joy Ministries in Liverpool

- Rev Siew Huat Ong, Senior Pastor of the Chinese Church in London

- Dr Samuel Cueva, Iglesia Misionera Evangelica

- Manoj Raithatha, National Coordinator of South Asian Forum (SAF)

- Rev Mike Talbot, vicar of Emmanuel Church Northwood and Chair of the Evangelical Alliance board

- Michael Puffett, Jubilee Church Maidstone

Other church leaders who have been part of this journey, among a host of others, include:

- Bishop John Francis, founder of Ruach Ministries

- Rev Obafemi Omisade, National Overseer of New Covenant Church

- Rev Dr Hugh Osgood, Senior Pastor of Cornerstone Christian Centre

- Bishop Wayne Malcolm, Senior Pastor Christian Life City

- Rev David Shosanya, London Baptist Association

- Pastor Kofi Banful, Senior Pastor of Praise Chapel

- Pastor Ade Omooba, co-founder of Christian Legal Centre (CLC) and Christian Concern for our Nation (CCFON)

From this list of the leaders involved, we can easily see that there is an overlap between the NCLF and the One People Commission. While they have different goals, they are in dialogue with each other, which was demonstrated at the already mentioned launch of the Black Church Political Manifesto on 14th March 2015, as Rev Yemi Adedeji was present to endorse the document. The One People Commission is a unique national initiative that brings together different church leaders with international perspectives and experiences in Britain. This group reflects what Harvey Kwiyani, a colleague of mine, describes as a 'multicultural missionary movement',[86] which is what is needed in a multicultural mission field and society such as the UK.

Churches Together in Britain and Ireland (CTBI) from the 1990s to the present

In 1990, the British Council of Churches changed its name and the way it operated. It became the Council of Churches in Britain and Ireland (CCBI), and later in 1999 became Churches Together in Britain and Ireland (CTBI). The change in operation was the result of a shift in focus from institutional ecumenism to facilitating relationships between member churches. In essence,

---

[86] Kwiyani, *Sent Forth*, pp.171-175.

the new body was to be understood as a way of helping churches to work together rather than on separate levels. This means that as an organisation it can speak and act only when there is consensus among the churches. The merging of the work of the Conference for Christian Partnership (CCP) into the Centre for Black and White Christian Partnership and the disbanding of the Zebra Project around the 1990s meant that some of the BMC could now work directly with the CCBI. The increase in the sharing of Historic Church buildings by BMC also facilitated and necessitated this change in direction of the work of CCBI, as greater attention was now being drawn to BMC.

Since the 1990s, CTE, one of the regional bodies of CTBI, has facilitated ecumenical conversations and engagement between BMC and Historic Churches, both nationally and locally. Nationally, it has done this since around 2003 through the work of Minority Ethnic Christian Affairs (MECA), now renamed Pentecostal and Multicultural Relations, led by Dr Joe Aldred. The work of MECA started under the presidency of Father Olu Abiola as one of the presidents of CCBI (now CTBI). This took place when the CAACC, being in membership of the Free Churches Federal Council, along with Rev David Staple who was then General Secretary of the Free Churches Council, helped to initiate a project called Black Christian Concern, which was later renamed Minority Ethnic Christian Affairs when the Free Churches group joined CTE.

MECA was created to help develop ecumenical relationships and engagement between BMC and Pentecostal churches (both white and black) with CTE. One result of this engagement has been the ongoing conversations between leaders of BMC and Historic Churches. For example, in January 2010 there was a consultation on Anglican relations with BMC. This consultation considered, among other things, how the Church of England can make its theological resources available for the benefit of ministerial training for BMC.[87] This is one clear example of the Historic Churches' privileged position and resources with regard to institutional ecumenism. The question can be asked, why cannot the Historic Churches also send some of their students to train at BMC Bible colleges? This could perhaps be arranged as an exchange programme.

Another national meeting was held in October 2010 at Lambeth Palace, and in attendance were leaders of BMC, Asian churches and Historic Churches. This meeting, in conjunction with MECA, was initiated by the joint presidents of CTE, including the former Archbishop of Canterbury, Dr Rowan Williams. The meeting, the first of its kind, considered how BMC and Historic Churches could work together in mission. It was stated that for this to happen, the following points were important for consideration:

- There is a need for a common and coherent voice which should be neither imperious nor imperial, and a new order of relationships among the leaders of the churches.

- There is a need for a platform of dialogue between the migrant and Historic Churches.

- We should begin with a vision of what God has done in Jesus, and we need to communicate more fully the richness of what God has done, and concentrate on those fundamental truths which unite us.

- We should seek to avoid the word 'denomination' and the baggage of 'denominationalism', because our churches are much more than labels. 'Denominations' look like clubs, and in a club we seek the company of people like us. All our

---

[87] 'Notes of a Consultation on Anglican Relations with Black Majority Churches', (London: Church House), 18th January 2010.

churches are more than that, and we need to discern the catholicity within each of them.

- The Historic Churches have not done enough to interact with the newer churches – links such as pulpit exchanges, sharing building resources and training need to be explored.[88]

This second meeting became more significant therefore because it acknowledged the privileged position that the Historic Churches have had with regard to ecumenism. In addition, the Historic Churches were willing to see BMC and Asian churches as equals.

These significant meetings between the Archbishop of Canterbury, the Catholic Archbishop for England and Wales and the heads of BMC have continued annually, and progress is being made. One of the significant steps that has been taken through this engagement is the appointment of Bishop Eric Brown, former National Overseer of New Testament Church of God, as the first Pentecostal joint president of CTE in 2013, making six presidents of CTE in total. These six presidents are:

- The Archbishop of Canterbury (Archbishop Justin Welby)

- The Cardinal Archbishop of Westminster (Cardinal Vincent Nichols)

- The Free Churches Moderator (Rev Dr Hugh Osgood, Churches in Communities)

- The President nominated by the New Churches, the Religious Society of Friends (the Quakers) and the Lutheran

---

[88] Minutes of meeting between the leaders of Black and Asian Majority Churches and the historic denominations, Lambeth Palace, 5th October 2010.

and German-speaking churches (Billy Kennedy, Pioneer Network)

- Representative of the Greek and Eastern Orthodox churches (Archbishop Gregorios of Thyateira and Great Britain)

- The Pentecostal President (Bishop Eric Brown)

Another important national conversation CTE and what is now Pentecostal and Multicultural Relations is facilitating is the Anglican Pentecostal Theological Consultation. This consultation explores the similarities and differences between the Church of England and black and white Pentecostal churches, and aims to chart a way forward for enhanced partnership in mission. One such meeting took place in April 2014, and in attendance were nine Anglicans and eight black and white Pentecostal theologians.[89]

Locally, CTE has facilitated ecumenical engagement through intermediary bodies such as Churches Together in South London (CTSL) and other Churches Together meetings and gatherings in different boroughs and areas of London. For example, in my previous church (Crofton Park Baptist Church), we were part of Brockley Churches Together which facilitated relationship between Anglicans, Baptists, BMC, Catholics, Indian Orthodox and Community churches. We held joint services on Good Fridays and Pentecost, and we worked together on mission projects such as Youth Alpha and Soul in the City.

Both the Evangelical Alliance and CTE continue to facilitate ecumenical dialogue and engagement. This has led to different churches doing mission together, while other activities have remained just a conversation. As CTE and the Evangelical Alliance continue national dialogues through the Archbishop of

---

[89] Minutes of Anglican Pentecostal Theological Consultation at High Leigh on 7th and 8th April 2014.

Canterbury's meetings with significant leaders of BMC and the One People Commission gatherings respectively, they continue to be examples of institutional ecumenism – that is, church unity through organisational structures.

Problems with institutional ecumenism

The first problem with institutional ecumenism is that Historic Churches continue to have the majority of the power and resources at their disposal. This means that the ecumenical instruments and agencies are still largely financed and controlled by Historic Churches.

The second problem is suspicion of the word 'ecumenism' by some BMC leaders. Some BMC leaders, being very evangelical and conservative in their theology, do not really want to work with Catholic churches or Spiritual churches, for example, and their leaders.[90] Their theology views some Historic Churches as either not Christian or not Spirit filled. In addition is the fact that some BMC leaders are not full-time paid pastors and therefore they might have two jobs – one as an unpaid pastor and the other in a secular job. This means that if local Churches Together meetings are held during the daytime, they may well not be able to attend and are therefore excluded.

A third problem is the lack of representation of BMC leaders in ecumenical posts and councils. I must emphasise that this is changing, as, for example, more and more BMC leaders are gradually becoming involved in CTE leadership. Here are some

---

[90] Spiritual churches are churches rooted in the cultural and traditional religious practices from Africa or the Caribbean. Examples will be some of the AIC in Africa and Spiritual Baptists from Trinidad. Syncretism, that is mixing elements of Traditional Religion and Christianity, is one of the major reasons why other Christians are sometimes suspicious of these churches.

examples of BMC leaders who have contributed and are still contributing to the ecumenical scene through CTBI and CTE:

- Father Olu Abiola, founder of Aladura International Church, was involved with the former BCC and became the first African to be one of the presidents of CCBI in the 1990s. He was fully involved in the inter-church process that led to the inauguration of the new ecumenical instrument from CCBI to CTBI and CTE respectively, and served on many of its committees.

- The late Rev Dr I. O. Smith, a leading member of New Testament Assembly, was actively involved with the work of Churches Together in Britain (when it was CCBI)

- Rev Nezling Sterling of New Testament Assembly, through CTBI (former joint president) and the Church of England's General Synod

- Rev Esme Beswick MBE, through CTE (former joint president)

- Bishop Eric Brown, first joint Pentecostal president of CTE

- Dr Joe Aldred, through Pentecostal and Multicultural Relations of CTE

- Bishop Donnett Thomas, through Churches Together in South London. She is currently the Chair of Churches Together in South London and a member of Ixthus Church Council

- Bishop Doye Agama, Director and Trustee of CTE and Moderator of the CTE Forum in 2015

Examples of local intercultural ecumenical partnerships

Having done a quick survey of the national ecumenical scene, let us now turn our attention to local ecumenism through the sharing of buildings and Spirit-led ecumenism which is seeing different churches working together in mission.

The sharing of church buildings of Historic Churches by BMC dates back to the 1960s. Many independent BMC who do not have their own buildings hire church halls or buildings from Historic Churches. The majority of these relationships over the years have remained as landlord and tenant. The minutes of one of the BCC meetings held in 1977 highlighted some of the problems BMC faced when hiring Historic Church buildings. These included large rents being charged, untidiness and poor state of the church hall or premises before use, strict observance of locking up church halls or premises, and suspicion of the BMC.[91] Malcolm Calley also observed in 1965 that Historic Churches were reluctant to let their halls because of the noise BMC were reputed to make, which often led to white residents complaining.[92]

Some of these problems and attitudes have changed over the years, and since the 1990s, some Historic Churches have taken further steps to be interested in their 'tenants'. It is worth mentioning that some Historic Churches have written documents or frameworks to facilitate and act as a guide on how to host other churches as guests rather than tenants. Examples of such documents are by the Anglican Diocese of Southwark,[93] 'Living Hospitably an Intercultural Journey' by the United

---

[91] BCC Division of Ecumenical Affairs, minutes of the first meeting of the Joint Working Party: Black-led and White-led Churches, held at St Philomena's Euston, 11th-12th March 1977.
[92] Elaine Foster, 'Out of this World: A Consideration of the Development and Nature of the Black-led Churches in Britain' in Paul Grant and Raj Patel (eds), *A Time to Speak: Perspectives of Black Christians in Britain* (Nottingham: Russell Press, 1990), p.62.
[93] Diocese of Southwark 2009.

Reformed Church[94] and the Baptist Union's 'Guidelines for Guest Congregations'.[95] While some of these guidelines help to spell out what is expected and what is not acceptable when hiring, some BMC hiring buildings also have to realise that not everyone appreciates the decibels that can be generated when worshipping God, or if they do not keep to time when they should. Some of these tensions have to be negotiated so that both parties can work together around the use of a building.

Some Historic Churches have more than just a landlord–tenant relationship with the BMC who share their church buildings, and some have managed to develop a working relationship. Here are listed some of the examples I have come across in South East London.

- Such a relationship existed between my previous church, Crofton Park Baptist Church, and a BMC para-church organisation called JUMP (Jesus Use My Potential). JUMP was a charity organisation that worked with disadvantaged black youths in the community.[96] It hired office premises from Crofton Park, but the relationship developed beyond just hiring and blossomed to having a joint youth house group. In addition, its young people, drawn from BMC such as KICC, New Testament Church of God and Church of God of Prophecy, also learnt about the Second World War from hearing stories told by the elderly people at Crofton Park. This was done through an elderly lunch club known as Welcome-Inn. Crofton Park now hosts another youth initiative free of charge, called Vessel Works. This is led by Ethan Bernard whose church background is New Testament

---

[94] 'Living Hospitably an Intercultural Journey: Newer Migrant Churches and The United Reformed Church', a document produced by the RJMM-Mission, United Reformed Church, October 2012.
[95] Baptist Union Council, 'Guidelines for Guest Congregations', 2011.
[96] JUMP sadly no longer exists as an organisation.

Church of God. Vessel Works is a volunteer-based, not-for-profit organisation that seeks to encourage, empower and equip young people through the use of music, media and mentoring, and is committed to helping young people think positively about what contributions they can make to our community and society.

- St Peter's Church in Brockley was a host to two BMC, one a Nigerian Pentecostal church (New Covenant Church) and the other a Caribbean Pentecostal church. New Covenant Church and St Peter's have held joint services on numerous occasions. This was made possible as the leaders of the two churches, Rev Dr John Omolafe of the New Covenant Church and Rev Corinne Tourney of St Peter's, decided to work together. At the heart of the relationship between the two churches was affirmation and respect for each other.[97]

- Another good example of ecumenical partnership in South East London through the sharing of buildings is in the borough of Southwark. This is between Haddon Hall Baptist Church in Bermondsey and House on the Rock (a Nigerian Pentecostal church). House on the Rock hires the church building from Haddon Hall, but they have also held joint services on numerous occasions. The relationship between Rev Carl Palmer of Haddon Hall and Pastor Lola Oyebade of House on the Rock is one of mutual respect.

- Another example is the relationship between an Asian church and a Baptist church in Lewisham. Brownhill Road Baptist Church is host to El-Bethel Tamil Church, which is led by Pastor Rajkumar and his wife, Rexy. Pastor Rajkumar and Rexy have regular fellowship with Rev Mike Kendal, the pastor of Brownhill Road Baptist Church. The two

---

[97] This particular New Covenant Church has now relocated to the Royal Borough of Greenwich.

churches, although very different in culture and theological world-view, have held joint watchnight services on New Year's Eve.

- Crossway United Reformed Church in Elephant and Castle is host to about eight different BMC. Rev Dr Peter Stevenson, the lead minister, is no longer seen as the landlord but as a friend by some of the guest churches. This change came about as a result of developing friendships with the pastors and holding joint services with some of the churches.[98]

- St Mary Magdalene Church in Woolwich, South East London, is host to Deeper Life Bible Church. Deeper Life Bible Church rents St Mary's church premises on Sunday afternoons for its services. It also rents office space for its weekly administration and midweek services. The churches have held a joint service and Rev Jessie van der Valk, minister of St Mary's, is a good host who is interested in his tenant.

Having mentioned some positive examples of churches sharing buildings, let us now look at some of the opportunities and challenges of such partnerships. This type of ecumenical partnership facilitates relationships on three levels:

1. Sharing of resources, such as church buildings and administrative skills.

2. Joint services and fellowship, house groups and prayer meetings.

3. Joint mission initiatives such as youth clubs, Street Pastors, food banks, immigration services and welfare for asylum seekers.

---

[98] 'Being Built Together', p.81.

Some of the challenges or difficulties people encounter in the sharing of buildings, or obstacles that prevent people from wanting to share buildings, are as follows:

- A superior attitude, where one thinks he or she is better than the other.

- Suspicion and lack of trust.

- Doctrinal and theological divides, such as Prosperity Gospel as articulated by some BMC, lack of centrality of Scripture of some Historic Churches as perceived by BMC.

- Ecclesiological divides – for example, Apostolic/ Pentecostal style of leadership as opposed to a congregational/ democratic style of leadership. Some BMC have strong leadership which can at times lead to abuse of power, while the democratic or consensus style of leadership can mean that the church takes forever to make decisions. Sometimes everything the leader or leadership team does is questioned to the extent that it betrays a lack of trust.

- Different views and understanding of mission: some BMC emphasise street evangelism as opposed to social and community engagement. This is changing, however, and now many BMC engage in both proclamation of the gospel and community and social action.

- Cultural divide: the use of indigenous languages by some BMC during services which excludes others who cannot speak that language. Other cultural divides include Harvest Festivals as practised by some Historic Churches which some other cultures cannot relate to or understand. Another cultural divide is the dress code for church on Sundays (the often formal dress code of black Christians and informal dress code of white Christians). This is obviously a stereotype as there are white pastors and Christians who like to dress formally to go to church and there are, equally, black Christians who like to dress in a more relaxed way.

How can these differences be overcome or negotiated?

- Mutual respect for one another and affirming equality
- Listening deeply to each other
- Awareness and respect of other theologies and doctrines, even if you do not agree with them
- Building relationships first before questioning doctrines or theology
- Willingness to embrace and learn from other cultures. This will need to go beyond lip service
- Having a kingdom theology that places God's mission at the heart of the agenda. God's mission is bigger than just one local church or church denomination, therefore we need each other to fulfil God's kingdom on earth
- Visiting each other's services and taking part in pulpit exchanges
- Not holding assumptions or preconceptions of people from cultures and churches that are different from ours
- Leaders speaking well of each other
- Spending time talking about what we agree on, rather than frowning on the differences

Having considered the sharing of buildings and the opportunities and challenges this generates, I want to look at two examples of how different churches in London are working together in mission. The first is a prayer initiative in South East London and the other is the relationship between Jesus House, Hillsong Church and Holy Trinity Brompton.

South East London Prayer Initiative

The South East London Prayer Initiative is led by Pastor Emmanuel Obi Eze and his wife, Pastor Jacqui, founders of the Guiding Light Church in Bromley. This prayer initiative started in around 2013 and attempts to bring together in prayer different churches in neighbouring boroughs in South East London. These boroughs include Bromley, Lewisham and Greenwich. The mission of the prayer initiative is to pray for revival in London. This is done through prayer walks, prayer gatherings, watchnight services and evangelism. The churches involved in this initiative include African Pentecostal churches, Caribbean Pentecostal churches, Church of England, Baptists and independent Charismatic churches. The South East London Prayer Initiative has also partnered with the South Korean prayer mission which brings South Korean missionaries annually into the UK for prayer and mission mobilisation. This kind of intercultural ecumenism lays emphasis on the work of the Holy Spirit through prayer in bringing together different people who are likeminded and who would like to see Britain experience renewal.

Trinitarian ecumenism: the case of Holy Trinity Brompton, Jesus House and Hillsong Church

Another fresh expression of ecumenism is seen where three or more churches have decided to come together to fellowship and do mission. This is not through any ecumenical institutions or through the sharing of buildings, but through the inspiration of the Holy Spirit. An example of this is the relationship that exists between Holy Trinity Brompton, Jesus House and Hillsong Church in London. Holy Trinity Brompton is an evangelical Anglican church known for its Alpha course. Jesus House is the national headquarters of the Redeemed Christian Church of God (RCCG) in London, which has its roots in Nigerian

Pentecostalism. Hillsong Church is a Pentecostal church from Australia. These three different churches have held concerts, conference gatherings and leadership conferences together and have participated in pulpit exchanges.

Their various gatherings have attracted thousands of Christians from across church denominations, such as the gathering at Pentecost 2012 at the O2 Arena. The service reflected the diversity and the gifting of the churches. Nicky Gumbel preached with his characteristic gentle persuasion; Gary Clarke, the leader of Hillsong Church, did the altar call; and Pastor Agu Irukwu gave an exaltation as well as collecting the offering. The Jesus House choir ministered alongside the worship team of Hillsong and the worship leaders of Holy Trinity Brompton. The three church leaders appear to be working on an equal partnership, and the churches did not try to outshine each other at the event. This Trinitarian ecumenism, if one may use the term, is speaking and inspiring other churches and church leaders to work together, particularly in London.

Emerging national unity movements

As congregations engage locally with other churches, either through the sharing of buildings, through mission initiatives such as food banks or through local networks such as Lewisham Churches United, new national unity movements are also emerging. These unity movements are resourcing local initiatives and networks through training, funding and facilitation. They are working across church denominations, not operating like national ecumenical institutions and organisations, but serving as movements enabling local church networks for mission. Two examples of such movements are Gather and the Cinnamon Network.

Gather started in recognition of the changing scene in ecumenism. Rather than having an organisation leading ecumenism, it is encouraging and supporting what local church networks are already doing. To this end, Gather's vision is to find out about local church networks in different cities and towns and to see how it can connect these vibrant and diverse local groupings together. Gather therefore views its role as a 'national network of vibrant missional unity movements in villages, towns and cities and boroughs' across the UK.[99] Gather works nationally but is perhaps more effective in the north of England in cities such as Manchester and Liverpool. The initiative is enabled by the Evangelical Alliance and led by Rev Roger Sutton and a team of strategic leaders.

The second initiative is the Cinnamon Network, which started in 2010 as a response to 'growing social need, public sector reform, increasing recognition of the role of voluntary organisations and the economic cuts'.[100] The founder of the network is Matt Bird who has coined the phrase 'Relationology' as a concept of building authentic relationships and friendships. One of the strengths of the Cinnamon Network is its ability to help local churches working together to access funds for mission projects such as CAP centres, Street Pastors, winter night shelters and food banks. It also facilitates networks and relationships of church leaders across denominations, cities, towns and regions. For example, in London it has facilitated the gathering of ecumenical borough deans from across the boroughs. In order to connect the work of the church with local authorities, some of these meetings have also connected the various borough deans and the borough police commanders.[101]

---

[99] See http://www.wegather.co.uk/ (accessed 11th February 2015).

[100] See http://www.cinnamonnetwork.co.uk/ (accessed 11th February 2015).

[101] Borough deans are church leaders representing the different church traditions in each borough in London. Usually, each borough will have a chair of borough deans who will be responsible for bringing together all the other borough deans in their area. A borough

Some of the significant things the Cinnamon Network did in 2015 include the Faith Action Audit, a survey that enabled local churches to document their stories of social and community engagement. The other, which I have already mentioned in chapter two, was the first Cinnamon Network Theology Symposium, with the theme of 'The Gospel, Social Action and Community Engagement'. The event, held at Emmanuel Centre in London, gathered together about 150 church leaders and mission practitioners from across the UK. The churches represented included BMC, Historic Churches and other church traditions. The symposium was chaired by Dr Lucy Peppiatt, Principal of Westminster Theological Centre, and the theme was addressed by three different theologians.

The first theological perspective was from a BMC Pentecostal church tradition, Rev David Shosanya, Baptist minister and co-founder of the Street Pastors initiative, whose spiritual and ministerial formation is rooted in Pentecostalism. Rev Shosanya continues to network within the Pentecostal constituency. The second theological perspective was from a Reformed Theologian, Dr Dan Strange, Vice-principal of Oakhill Theological College. The third theological perspective was from a Charismatic evangelical, Dr Mark Bonnington, a New Testament scholar at Cranmer Hall, Durham, and leader of an independent Charismatic church, King's Church in Durham.

The purpose of the symposium was to equip pastors and mission practitioners with a strong mission theology that leads to holistic mission practice. In essence, theological reflection was seen as crucial to engaging communities with the gospel, either through social-political action or gospel proclamation (evangelism). Having Rev Shosanya representing the theological perspective of black Pentecostal churches on social political

commander is a senior police officer in charge of policing in that borough.

action demonstrates that the Cinnamon Network takes intercultural ecumenism seriously.

The Network also has BMC leaders as part of its overall leadership team and governance. These include Pastor Girma Bishaw, Senior Pastor of Ethiopian Fellowship Church in London, who is part of the Cinnamon Network advisory council; and Bishop Wayne Malcolm, Senior Pastor of Christian Life City in London, who is on the board of trustees. In addition, the Network has also developed good working relationships with key BMC, which is why some BMC leaders were present at the theology symposium.

These new national ecumenical movements are responding to the changes in missional ecumenism and society. While they are national in outlook, their strength is in connecting and resourcing what local church networks are already doing. They are new forms of institutional ecumenism, but with the recognition and understanding that building relationships with local church leaders is the way forward and the future of ecumenism in Britain. They are also focused on mission rather than on leaders gathering for the purpose of relationship building.

Towards an intercultural ecumenical future: a way forward

Where do we go from here? In this section is a summary of my key points, drawing implications for future study and the future of mission and ecumenism in Britain.

This short book has made three main points, the first of which is that BMC are a significant part of the British church and its history. A contention of this book is that we need to rethink what we mean by BMC. Another way of understanding the term BMC is Black Multicultural Churches, as this reflects the diversity that exists within some of these churches. It is a diverse church movement, hence the need to consider a change of the term

106

because 'Black Majority Churches' is certainly not describing the rich diversity that exists within these churches.

The second point is that BMC have travelled a long way from being migrant sanctuaries and are on their way towards structural change. There have been certain theological developments along the way that have mapped out this significant journey. These include the understanding that Britain is a mission field, and the desire to change from mono-ethnic churches to multicultural churches. The latter has led to various approaches such as collaborative mission strategies, the development of missional church conversations, and social and community engagement. While BMC are still on a journey, there are signs such as the Political Manifesto that are pointing in the right direction.

In order to achieve political consciousness that changes structures, BMC will have to develop mission theology or engage and listen to their resident theologians, be prophetic and engage in strategic partnership that demonstrates equality. Ubuntu philosophy, which understands our humanity in terms of a shared identity, was used to reconstruct Prosperity Gospel as a plausible holistic mission theology that could transform society. This could be achieved if Prosperity Gospel were to change its emphasis from that of individual consumerism to benefiting the wider community. This is called Commonwealth Gospel, which makes wealth common to everyone!

Lastly, there is a new intercultural ecumenism emerging between BMC and Historic Churches. This intercultural ecumenism is happening both nationally and locally. Attention is drawn to what is happening in different parts of London in particular, some through the sharing of church buildings and others through the leading of the Spirit into mission.

What implications do these have for the future of mission and ecumenism in Britain? As a result of the growth and mission of BMC, particularly those that are denominations, some have now acquired their own church buildings. We are now therefore seeing BMC hiring from other BMC, and independent white-led churches hiring from BMC. I suspect more BMC will continue to buy their own church buildings, but there is a problem of lack of industrial warehouse buildings to buy, as well as limitations and restrictions of buildings for church use. This situation will force BMC to either adapt and move to rural areas or go the way of fresh expressions of church, such as doing church in pubs, cafés and other neutral spaces. Adapting to any of these scenarios will require a lot of contextualisation and rethinking of what is mission.

From the discussion in chapter two on how some BMC are engaging in conversations on developing missional communities, it is possible that some would consider venturing into fresh expressions of church. However, as it is early days, what I suspect will happen (because many BMC still struggle with the idea of doing church in a pub, a café and so on) is that they will continue to seek to hire church halls, schools and community centres in urban areas. This means they will have to work on their relationships with Historic Churches, paying attention to issues such as noise, time management and parking. They will have to do the same when renting schools and community centres, as I am aware that many of these institutions do not want to rent out their buildings to BMC because of such issues.

Another implication is that if BMC have now become one of the largest and fastest-growing segments of the church in Britain, and if Historic Churches continue to decline, this begs the question of who will hold the ecumenical resources and power in the future. One of the strengths of BMC is the giving attitude of their members, which means that these churches hold substantial financial power. Some are able to purchase massive warehouses without a mortgage because of the wealth they have. If this continues, then ecumenical agencies and bodies may well come to need resources from BMC. This could lead to change in institutional ecumenism and the way it is operated. (One clarification here is that not all Historic Churches are experiencing decline, and some are experiencing growth![102])

A third implication is that as churches continue to work together around mission projects and Spirit-led ecumenism, there is a question as to what role ecumenical agencies such as CTE will play. I suspect CTE will have to adapt again as it did in the 1990s, so that it becomes an instrument that facilitates and resources some of these mission projects. However, a further pressing question is, if grassroots intercultural ecumenism is emerging all over, do we still need national ecumenical agencies? And if so, what role will they play? I think for the time being we still need agencies such as the Evangelical Alliance to facilitate some of those national conversations and dialogue, through groups such as the One People Commission. How long they will be needed is an open question for the future.

The Gather initiative of the Evangelical Alliance is one way in which the Alliance is adapting and recognising the changing pattern in ecumenism, but more work still needs to be done to involve more BMC. Gather's working and partnering with local churches and networks to facilitate more connections between cities and towns across the UK is welcomed, and its efforts and those of the Cinnamon Network might be what the future of institutional ecumenism looks like: an ecumenism that gives more support, finance and resources to grassroots networks of local churches.

Whatever the future looks like, God's creative Spirit will continue to hover and move in various ways to bring different churches together to work for His kingdom. Indeed, as we

---

102 David Goodhew (ed), *Church Growth in Britain: 1980 to the Present* (Surrey: Ashgate Publishing Limited, 2012), pp.3-6.

continue into the future, the role of the Spirit in intercultural mission and ecumenism becomes more crucial and significant!

Select bibliography on BMC in Britain

Adedibu, Babatunde, *Coat of Many Colours: The Origin, Growth, Distinctiveness and Contributions of Black Majority Churches to British Christianity*, London: Wisdom Summit, 2012.

Adogame, Afe, *The African Christian Diaspora: New Currents and Emerging Trends in World Christianity*, London: Bloomsbury Academic, 2013.

Aldred, Joe, *Respect: Understanding Caribbean British Christianity*, Werrington, Peterborough: Epworth Publishers, 2005.

Aldred, Joe and Ogbo, Keno (eds), *The Black Church in the 21st Century*, London: Darton, Longman & Todd Ltd, 2010.

Beckford, Robert, *Dread and Pentecostalism: A Political Theology for the Black Church in Britain*, London: SPCK, 2000.

Beckford, Robert, *Jesus is Dread: Black Theology and Black Culture in Britain*, London: Darton, Longman & Todd Ltd, 1998.

Chike, Chigor, *African Christianity in Britain*, Milton Keynes: Author House, 2007.

Chike, Chigor, *Holy Spirit in African Christianity: An Empirical Study*, Milton Keynes: Authentic Media, 2015.

Edwards, Joel (ed), *Let's Praise Him Again: An African-Caribbean Perspective on Worship*, Eastbourne: Kingsway Publications Ltd, 1992.

Gerloff, Roswith, *A Plea for British Black Theology: The Black Church Movement in Britain in its Transatlantic Cultural and Theological Interaction with Oneness (Apostolic) and Sabbatarian Movements* Vol 1, Eugene, Oregon: Wipf and Stock Publishers, 2010.

Gerloff, Roswith and other contributors, 'Partnership in Black and White', a publication of the Methodist Church Home Mission Division, 1977.

Grant, Paul and Patel, Raj (eds), *A Time to Speak: Perspectives of Black Christians in Britain*, Birmingham: CRRU/ECRJ, 1990.

Harris, Hermoine, *Yoruba in Diaspora: An African Church in London*, New York: Palgrave Macmillan, 2006.

Hill, Clifford, 'Black Churches: West Indian and African Sects in Britain', London, Community and Race Relations Unit of the British Council of Churches, 1971.

Hollenweger, Walter, *The Pentecostals*, London: SCM Press Ltd, 1972.

Jagessar, Michael and Reddie Anthony (eds), *Black Theology in Britain*, London: Equinox Publishing Ltd, 2007.

Kalu, Ogbu (ed), *African Christianity: An African Story*, Trenton, NJ, African World Press, 2007.

Kerridge, Roy, *The Storm is Passing Over: A Look at Black Churches in Britain*, London: Thames and Hudson, 1995.

Killingray, David and Edwards, Joel, *Black Voices: The Shaping of our Christian Experience*, Nottingham: Inter-Varsity Press, 2007.

Kwiyani, Harvey, *Sent Forth: African Missionary Work in the West*, New York: Orbis Books, 2014.

London Borough of Southwark, 'Being Built Together: A Story of New Black Majority Churches in the London Borough of Southwark', Final Report, June 2013.

Mohabir, Philip, *Building Bridges*, London: Hodder & Stoughton, 1988.

Olofinjana, Israel, *Reverse in Ministry and Missions: Africans in the Dark Continent of Europe*, Milton Keynes: Author House, 2010.

Olofinjana, Israel, *Turning the Tables: Stories of Christians from the Global South in the UK*, Watford, Instant Apostle, 2013.

Reddie, Richard, *From an Acorn to an Oak Tree: The History of the New Testament Assembly in the UK*, London: New Testament Assembly, 2012.

Sturge, Mark, *Look What the Lord has Done: An Exploration of Black Christian Faith in Britain*, Milton Keynes: Scripture Union, 2005.

About Centre for Missionaries from the Majority World

www.cmmw.co.uk

Centre for Missionaries
from the
Majority
World

Centre for Missionaries from the Majority World is a network/training hub that aims to prepare, equip and encourage pastors and missionaries from the Majority World in Britain as well as help indigenous British Christians and churches understand Christians from the South.

Vision and objectives

1. To prepare, equip and encourage pastors and missionaries from the Majority World in Britain and other parts of Europe to understand the postmodern secular context of European societies and culture.

2. To encourage southern scholarship and publications through books, journals and other forms of academic materials in order to develop a strong theology of mission that is practical and will help the next generation of mission practitioners from the Majority World.

3. To help British indigenous Christians and church leaders understand the mission and theology of Christians from the Majority World so as to improve relationships. Part of the learning will be to help British indigenous Christians understand the background of these missionaries.

4. To help pastors and missionaries who are interested in church planting to find out where a church plant might be

needed. This will avoid several churches being planted in the same proximity. It will involve networking and research to make information available in terms of where churches, mission initiatives or projects might be best needed in order to avoid competition and waste of resources that could be diverted to the right places at the right time.

History

- October 2013: the Centre as well as a book resource (*Turning the Tables on Mission: Stories of Christians from the Global South in Britain*) was launched at the Evangelical Alliance headquarters by Steve Clifford.

- March–May 2014: missional conversations once a month for three months attended by different church leaders and held at Brockley Baptist Church in London.

- September 2014: in partnership with Spurgeon's College, South Asian Forum (SAF), South Asian Concern (SAC) and One People Commission, a one-day conference was held, exploring the theme 'Partnership in Mission'.

- March 2015: in partnership with the Ethiopian Church and the Evangelical Alliance, another one-day conference was held, exploring multicultural, multi-ethnic churches.

The team

Dr Harvey Kwiyani is an emerging younger-generation African missiologist who has spent more than ten years working as a scholar and a practitioner in missions in Europe and North America. He graduated with a PhD from Luther Seminary in 2012, having researched the theological implications of the missionary work of Africans in North America. Harvey has published some of his research findings in his new book, *Sent*

Forth: African Missionary Work in the West (2014, Orbis Books). He teaches missions, leadership, and African studies at Birmingham Christian College and at the Church Mission Society (CMS) in Oxford. He is also a research fellow at the Cuddesdon Study Centre at Ripon College, Cuddesdon.

Peter Oyugi hails from Kenya and currently works for AIM International as the Area Mobiliser for South England and South Wales. He previously served as pastor of a church in North West London and also as a student worker among university and college students in both Kenya and the UK. Peter regularly teaches the Bible at IFES conferences in English-speaking Africa. He has a passion for cross-cultural mission that has grown out of being exposed to different cultures from childhood. His father is Kenyan and his mother is Finnish. Peter is an avid sports lover and takes a keen interest in African politics. He is married to Cecilia and they have two daughters.

Tayo Arikawe is a missionary and Bible teacher. One of his recent interests is reverse/inverse mission with a view to building multicultural churches that will reach out to the lost in the continent of Europe. He is the international director of Grace Evangelistic Ministries Europe (GEM), a non-denominational Bible teaching missionary organisation whose first priority is to take the gospel of grace to a lost and dying world. The ministry operates in more than 60 countries of the world. Tayo completed an MTh from the University of Chester via the Wales Evangelical School of Theology. He also holds a BSc in Geology and Mineral Science from the University of Ilorin, Nigeria. On a good day, he can be found at the gym. He is married to Calista and they are blessed with a son, Mekus.

Dr Samuel Cueva is a Peruvian missiologist whose PhD explored partnership in mission between Western Churches and Latin American Churches. His PhD has been published as a book, *Mission Partnership in Creative Tension*, published by Langham Monographs (2015). Samuel is the pastor of a Spanish-speaking church, Iglesia Misionera Evangelica, in North London and founder and President of Mission for the Third Millennium. He is also a member of the Evangelical Alliance One People Commission and Latin American Core Group. He is a regular speaker at national and international conferences.

Rev Israel Oluwole Olofinjana is an ordained and accredited Baptist minister who has pastored Crofton Park Baptist Church (2007–11) and Catford Community Church (2011–13). He is currently the pastor of Woolwich Central Baptist Church, a Black Majority Multicultural Church in South East London. He is Nigerian, from a Pentecostal background. He holds a BA (Hons) in Religious Studies from the University of Ibadan, Nigeria and an MTh from Carolina University of Theology (CUT). Israel is the editor of *Turning the Tables on Mission: Stories of Christians from the Global South in the UK, Reverse in Ministry and Missions: Africans in the Dark Continent of Europe* and *20 Pentecostal Pioneers in Nigeria*. He has spoken at a number of conferences on the subject of reverse mission and BMC, and has contributed to academic materials and Christian magazines on the subject of BMC in Britain. He is a co-opted member of the Baptist Union Council. Israel is also a member of the Global Connections Council. He is happily married to Lucy who works for the Evangelical Alliance in their mission and unity department.

Partners

- Global Connections: we have a working relationship with Global Connections, who support us administratively and in other ways
- South Asian Forum (SAF)
- South Asian Concern (SAC)